The Art Lover's Cookbook

A Feast for the Eye

Fine Arts Museums
of San Francisco

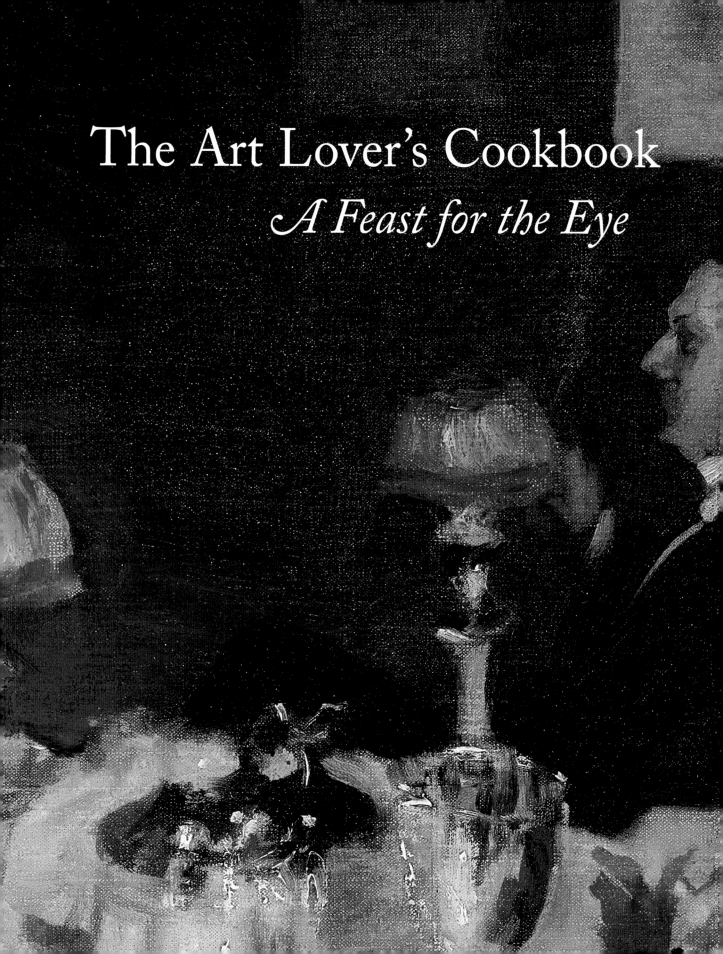

The Art Lover's Cookbook
A Feast for the Eye

The Art Lover's Cookbook: A Feast for the Eye
Published upon the occasion of the exhibition
A Feast for the Eye: Food in Art
M. H. de Young Memorial Museum
September 26–December 13, 1998

ISBN 0-88401-096-1
Library of Congress Catalog Card Number 98-72923

FINE ARTS MUSEUMS OF SAN FRANCISCO

M. H. de Young Memorial Museum
75 Tea Garden Drive, Golden Gate Park
San Francisco, CA 94118

California Palace of the Legion of Honor
100 - 34th Avenue, Lincoln Park
San Francisco, CA 94121

*Additional copies of this book may be ordered from the
Museum Stores, M. H. de Young Memorial Museum:
(415) 750-7649 (retail); (415) 750-3606 (wholesale).*

Front cover: William J. McCloskey, *Oranges in
Tissue Paper* (detail), ca. 1890

Title page: John Singer Sargent, *A Dinner Table
at Night (The Glass of Claret)* (detail), 1884

Back cover flap: Ken Price, *Untitled,* second plate
from the portfolio *Heat Wave,* 1995

Photographs from the Fine Arts Museums of
San Francisco: Joseph McDonald, Photographer
Photo credit: p. 46 Edward Weston, *Cabbage,*
© 1981 Center for Creative Photography, Arizona
Board of Regents

Produced through the Publications Department
of the Fine Arts Museums of San Francisco:
Ann Heath Karlstrom, Director of Publications,
and Karen Kevorkian, Managing Editor

Copyediting by Carolyn Miller
Index by Frances Bowles
Designed by Susan E. Kelly
Produced by Marquand Books, Inc., Seattle
Printed and bound by CS Graphics Pte. Ltd.,
Singapore

Contents

Foreword

The delicious and varied recipes in *The Art Lover's Cookbook: A Feast for the Eye* are gifts from the staff, docents, volunteers, visitors, and friends of the Fine Arts Museums of San Francisco. They represent the rich amalgam of many nationalities and traditions that have found a place on the West Coast of this country.

The accompanying images drawn from the Museums' collections illustrate the amusing and complicated relationships we have with food, our sustenance and our delight. Scenes of intimate dinners, simple communal meals, glorious banquets, and the various means of food's presentation underscore its celebratory, ritual, and social natures. The still lifes, genre scenes, cartoons, photographs, and decorative arts that illustrate these recipes reflect both the serious and the humorous sides of food in all its permutations.

The Art Lover's Cookbook is published to coincide with the exhibition *A Feast for the Eye* at the M. H. de Young Memorial Museum, and most of the works pictured in the book are presented in the exhibition. In our many cultures, food has been a complex form of expression and often the subject of great artistry and creativity. We hope you enjoy tasting and reflecting on these expressions in both of the Museums' presentations.

Harry S. Parker III
Director of Museums

Charles Sheeler, *Kitchen, Williamsburg,* 1937

Appetizers

:: *Blue Potato Bijoux* ::

6 large Peruvian blue (or purple)
   potatoes cut into ⅜-inch slices
½ teaspoon saffron threads
2 tablespoons boiling water
4 hard-cooked egg yolks
1 heaping tablespoon mayonnaise,
   or more as needed
Salt and freshly ground pepper to taste
Red caviar or flying fish roe for garnish

These are sensational on a black tray.

Cook the potatoes in salted boiling water for 8 to 10 minutes, or until they can be pierced with a fork; drain and let cool. Cut the cooled potatoes into star or flower shapes with cookie cutters. Grind the saffron threads in a mortar, or in a cup with the back of a spoon. Pour the boiling water over the saffron and let stand for about 15 minutes. Strain the liquid.

Mash the egg yolks, mayonnaise, and saffron water together. Add the salt and pepper. Add a little more mayonnaise, if necessary, to make a smooth mixture.

Using a pastry bag fitted with a star tip, pipe a small mound of the egg yolk mixture onto each potato piece. Garnish with a sprinkle of caviar or roe.

MAKES ABOUT 24 PIECES

Note: When buying blue potatoes, look for the ones with the most-veined skins; they will have the darkest blue insides. Also, keep the leftover saffron water and add it to rice or sauces for color.

:: *Marinated Mushrooms* ::

⅓ cup red wine vinegar
⅔ cup olive or vegetable oil
1 tablespoon chopped fresh parsley
½ teaspoon salt
½ teaspoon freshly ground pepper
½ teaspoon sugar
1 tablespoon fresh lemon juice
1 garlic clove
2 pounds small mushrooms, stemmed

Combine all the ingredients except the garlic and mushrooms in a big jar and mix well. Add the garlic and mushrooms. Refrigerate for several days; turn the jar occasionally. Remove the garlic and serve the mushrooms on toothpicks.

MAKES 2 POUNDS MUSHROOMS

PAGE 8 Albrecht Dürer, *Adam and Eve,* 1504

:: *Szechuan Brussels Sprouts and Mushrooms* ::

24 Brussels sprouts of even size
12 large white mushrooms, quartered
  lengthwise
⅓ cup Asian (toasted) sesame oil
1 tablespoon red pepper flakes
1 tablespoon sesame seeds
1 small carrot, peeled
¼ cup soy sauce or to taste
2 tablespoons minced fresh cilantro

Cook the Brussels sprouts in salted boiling water until just tender. Do not overcook. Drain. Place the mushrooms in a large bowl. In a small saucepan, heat the sesame oil until a drop of water sputters. Immediately remove from heat and add the pepper flakes. Be careful not to breathe in the fumes.

Cut the warm Brussels sprouts in half lengthwise and add to the mushrooms. Strain the chili oil over all and toss to coat.

In a dry skillet over medium-high heat, toast the sesame seeds and add to the sprouts. With a vegetable peeler, make carrot "curls." Add the carrot and cilantro to the salad and toss to mix. Let stand for 1 hour or so before serving, tossing a few times. Add the soy sauce just before serving. Garnish with cilantro and serve with toothpicks.

SERVES 8

:: *Roasted Red Peppers* ::

3 red bell peppers
2 tablespoons or more extra virgin
  olive oil
1 teaspoon cumin seed, or to taste
French bread for serving

Any leftovers make a nice garnish for omelettes or an interesting addition to a variety of sauces for pasta.

Blister the peppers under the broiler, turning as necessary until their skins are nicely blackened all over. Drop the peppers into a clean brown paper bag to cool to the touch. Peel, core, and seed the peppers, and chop them into bite-sized pieces. Put the chopped peppers in a serving dish, drizzle them with olive oil, and sprinkle with cumin seed. Mix lightly. Serve mounded on sliced French bread.

SERVES 6

:: *Eggplant and Pepper Caponata* ::

6 Japanese eggplants
2 red bell peppers
2 yellow bell peppers
2 tablespoons balsamic vinegar
¼ cup olive oil
¼ teaspoon cayenne pepper
1 bunch flat-leaf (Italian) parsley,
  stemmed and minced

A colorful appetizer given a wonderful roasted flavor by the grilled vegetables. Toasted garlic bread is a delicious pairing, along with Pinot Noir.

Light a fire in a charcoal grill or preheat a gas grill. Prick each eggplant all over 4 or 5 times. Grill over a hot fire until blackened and steaming. Remove. Grill the red and yellow peppers until evenly blackened. Place them in a paper bag to steam for 20 minutes. Peel the eggplant and cut into 1½-inch slices. Peel and seed the peppers and cut into 1½-inch slices. Whisk the vinegar, oil, and cayenne together. Toss with the eggplant and peppers. Let stand for 2 to 3 hours or refrigerate overnight. Sprinkle with parsley and serve at room temperature.

SERVES 4

:: *Szechuan Dip* ::

2 tablespoons chopped garlic
3 tablespoons chopped fresh cilantro
½ cup unsalted peanut butter
½ cup plus 1 tablespoon soy sauce
1 to 2 tablespoons chili oil
3 tablespoons sugar
1 teaspoon rice wine vinegar

Serve this as dip with snow peas, endive leaves, or red pepper strips, or as a sauce for stir-fries.

Mince the garlic in a blender. Add all the remaining ingredients and blend until smooth. Refrigerate for at least 1 hour or up to 1 week.

MAKES 1 CUP

Anonymous, Japanese, *Radishes and Summer Herbs*, ca. 1820–35

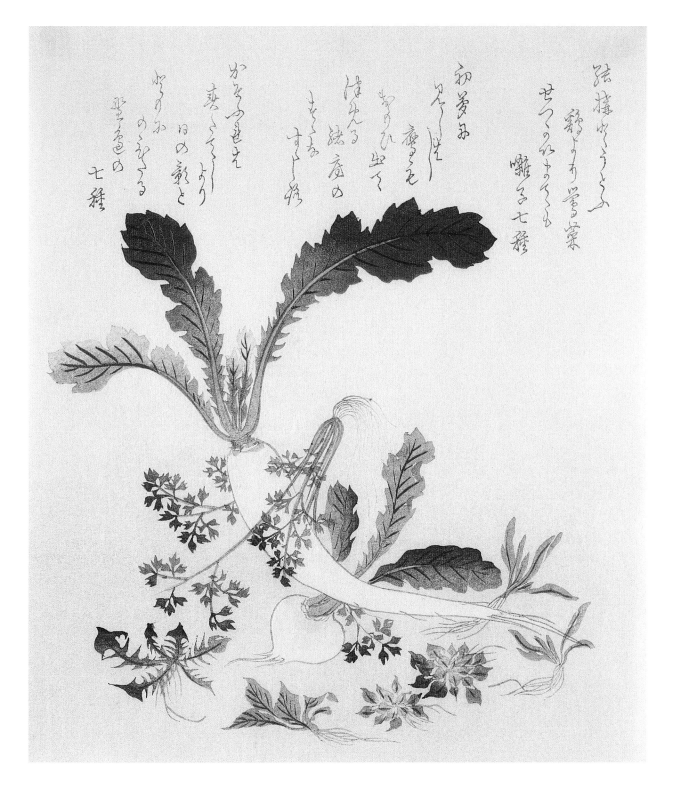

:: *Brazilian Hors d'Oeuvres* ::

1 banana, peeled
1 pound unpitted prunes
Thinly sliced bacon

Preheat the oven to 375°F. Cut the banana into ¼-inch slices, then cut these in half. Remove the pits from prunes by opening them on one side. Place a piece of banana inside each prune. Wrap each prune with ⅓ of a strip of bacon and secure with a toothpick. Bake for 15 minutes, or until the bacon is crisp.

MAKES ABOUT 40 PIECES

:: *Eggplant Dip* ::

1 large eggplant
¼ cup tahini
Juice of 2 lemons
3 green onions, finely chopped
1 garlic clove, minced
½ teaspoon ground cumin
¼ teaspoon cayenne pepper, or
  1 jalapeño chili, minced (optional)
Olive oil for topping
3 tablespoons chopped fresh parsley

This Middle Eastern dip can be served with raw vegetables, warm pita bread, or crackers.

Preheat the oven to 450°F. Puncture the eggplant with a fork or knife in several places. Place in a pie pan or on a baking sheet and bake for 30 to 45 minutes, or until soft. Cut the eggplant in half and remove the soft flesh, discarding the skin. Mash the eggplant in a bowl. Mix in the tahini and then the lemon juice. Add the green onions, garlic, cumin, and cayenne or jalapeño. Refrigerate for at least 1 hour. Serve the dip on a platter, drizzled with olive oil and sprinkled with parsley.

SERVES 4 TO 6

Wallpaper printed by Joseph Dufour,
The Voyages of Captain Cook (detail),
1804–6

:: *Phyllo-Wrapped Japanese Eggplant* ::

1 Japanese eggplant, cut into ⅛-inch-
    thick lengthwise slices
2 tablespoons soy sauce
1½ tablespoons corn oil
1 teaspoon grated fresh ginger
2 garlic cloves, crushed
10 sheets frozen phyllo dough, thawed
½ cup (1 stick) butter, melted

A pleasant, tangy appetizer

Preheat the oven to 400°F. Cut the sliced eggplant into
1-inch pieces. Combine the soy sauce, oil, ginger, and
garlic in a large bowl. Add the eggplant and toss gently
to coat. Arrange on a baking sheet in a single layer. Bake
until browned, about 15 minutes. Let cool.

Lightly grease a baking sheet. Cut 1 phyllo sheet
into 2 × 12-inch strips. Keep the remaining phyllo covered with a damp cloth. Brush 1 strip with butter. Place
1 piece of eggplant onto the end of the strip. Fold up flag
fashion. Repeat with the remaining strips and sheets.
The pieces can be refrigerated or frozen at this point;
thaw before baking. Brush lightly with butter. Reduce
the oven temperature to 350°F. and bake the eggplant
until golden brown, about 15 minutes.

MAKES 36 PIECES

:: *Spinach and Mushroom Frittatas* ::

10 tablespoons butter
¾ pound mushrooms, sliced
5 medium shallots, minced
4 large garlic cloves, minced
20 ounces frozen spinach, thawed,
  chopped, and squeezed dry
8 eggs, beaten
1¼ cups (5 ounces) grated Parmesan
  cheese
1 to 1¼ teaspoons salt, depending on
  saltiness of the cheese
½ teaspoon freshly ground pepper

Preheat the oven to 400°F. Melt 6 tablespoons of the butter in a large skillet, over medium heat. Add the mushrooms, shallots, and garlic. Sauté until the liquid is nearly evaporated. Reduce heat, add the spinach, and sauté for 2 minutes, being careful not to let the spinach brown. Remove from heat and set aside.

Combine the eggs and 1 cup of the cheese. Add the spinach mixture, salt, and pepper. Mix well. Melt the remaining 4 tablespoons butter and use to coat a 10-inch pie plate or an 8 × 11-inch baking pan. Fill the baking dish and sprinkle remaining cheese on top. Bake for 15 to 20 minutes, or until set. Cut into small squares or diamonds to serve.

MAKES 24 TO 30 APPETIZERS

:: *Onion and Bacon Tart with Framboise* ::

½ pound pancetta or bacon, cut into
  ½-inch squares
6 medium white onions
4 tablespoons butter
Salt and freshly ground pepper to taste
1 cup heavy cream
¼ cup framboise eau-de-vie
One 10-inch round pizza dough, made
  with rendered pancetta or bacon fat
  instead of oil

This is an original recipe by Chef Robert Reynolds.

Slowly render the pancetta or bacon in a skillet just to the point of browning. Remove with a slotted spoon and set aside. Cut the onions in half lengthwise and cut crosswise into ¼-inch slices. Add the butter to the skillet in which the pancetta was rendered and sauté the onions with a little salt until translucent. Grind fresh pepper over the onions and let cool. Stir the cream and eau-de-vie into the onions. Place the dough on an oiled pizza pan. Cover the dough with the onion-cream mixture, then garnish with pancetta pieces. Bake for 30 to 40 minutes, or until lightly browned.

SERVES 6

:: *Mushroom Tarts with Walnut Cream* ::

PASTRY

1⅓ cups all-purpose flour

Pinch of salt

7 tablespoons cold butter, chopped

2 to 4 tablespoons ice water

FILLING

1 pound small porcini, morels, or other flavorful mushrooms, thinly sliced

½ cup (2 ounces) walnuts

2 ounces prosciutto

1 egg

1⅓ cups bread cubes, soaked in ⅓ cup milk and squeezed dry

1 shallot, minced and sautéed lightly in butter

½ cup heavy cream

Salt and freshly ground pepper to taste

2 tablespoons melted butter

1 tablespoon walnut oil

1 garlic clove, crushed

This recipe takes a little work, but it is well worth the effort. Serve the rich and earthy tarts as the first course for a dinner of roasted game or beef.

Three to 4 hours before serving, make the pastry: Combine the flour and salt in a food processor and pulse to blend. Add the chopped butter and pulse until the texture resembles coarse meal. Add water as needed until the dough just holds together; do not overwork.

To make by hand, stir the flour and salt together in a bowl. Using a pastry cutter or 2 knives cut in the butter to the texture of coarse meal. Stir in the water until the dry ingredients are moistened. Form into a ball.

Turn the dough out onto plastic wrap and shape into a disk, wrap tightly, and refrigerate for 3 to 4 hours. Roll out very thin between 2 pieces of plastic. Line eight 4-inch round tart pans and refrigerate until ready to use.

To make the filling: Preheat the oven to 400°F. Blanch the mushrooms in salted boiling water for 5 minutes. Drain and pat dry with paper towels. Finely chop the walnuts in a food processor or blender. Add the prosciutto, egg, bread, and shallot and puree into a paste. Refrigerate for 30 minutes.

Gradually work the cream into the walnut mixture with a fork. Add salt and pepper. Spread a thin, even layer of walnut mixture over the dough in each tart pan. Fan the mushrooms over the surface. Mix the melted butter, walnut oil, garlic, and salt and pepper to taste together and brush the mushrooms lightly. Bake for 25 to 30 minutes, or until lightly browned. Serve hot.

SERVES 8

:: *Canlis's Shrimps* ::

2 pounds jumbo shrimp, shelled
  and deveined
1 tablespoon butter
1 tablespoon olive oil
1 small garlic clove, crushed
¼ teaspoon salt
¼ teaspoon freshly ground pepper
Juice of 2 lemons
¼ cup dry vermouth

This recipe comes from Canlis's restaurant, formerly in San Francisco.

In a large skillet over medium heat, heat the olive oil to simmering and sauté the shrimp until pink and opaque, 3 to 4 minutes. Reduce heat to low and add the butter, oil, garlic, salt, and pepper. Increase heat to high, add the lemon juice and vermouth, and cook for 1 minute, stirring constantly.

SERVES 6 TO 8

:: *Shrimp "Ceviche"* ::

1¼ pounds medium shrimp
1 heaping teaspoon salt
¼ teaspoon red pepper flakes
4 teaspoons ground allspice
½ cup finely chopped onion
⅓ cup olive oil
Grated zest of ½ lime
1½ cups fresh lime juice
¼ cup chopped fresh cilantro
2 green or red Anaheim chilies,
  seeded and chopped
2 heaping teaspoons minced garlic
1 teaspoon dried Greek oregano

This excellent dish is from Portugal. Although it's similar to ceviche, here the shrimp is cooked, then marinated.

Place the shrimp in a saucepan of cold water. Add the salt, pepper flakes, and allspice. Cover and bring to a boil. Reduce heat and simmer for 30 seconds. Remove from heat and let cool. Drain, shell, and devein the shrimp.

Put the shrimp in a bowl and add all the remaining ingredients. Cover tightly and refrigerate for 1 to 2 hours. Serve cold or at room temperature.

SERVES 8 TO 10

:: *"Drunken" Clams* ::

8 to 10 large cherrystone clams
½ bottle sake (Japanese rice wine)
2 limes
1 tablespoon salt
1 teaspoon ground pepper

Serve these with white wine.

Soak the clams in a pot of saltwater for 2 hours. Pour off the water. Pour the sake into the pot over the clams and let them marinate for 3 to 4 hours or overnight in the refrigerator.

Light a fire in a charcoal grill or preheat a gas grill. Grill the clams over a hot fire until they open; discard any clams that do not open. Squeeze the limes into a shallow bowl. Add the clams, salt, and pepper and mix well.

SERVES 2 TO 4

:: *Beef Jerky* ::

2¼ pounds flank steak, trimmed of fat
2 teaspoons seasoned salt
2 teaspoons liquid smoke (optional)
1 garlic clove, crushed
1 teaspoon chili powder
2 teaspoons Worcestershire sauce
½ cup soy sauce
1½ teaspoons garlic powder
¾ cup bourbon

Keep jerky in a self-sealing plastic bag in your shirt pocket when hiking in the great outdoors and eat at the first sign of hunger pangs. Or serve with beer while watching a game on television.

Partially freeze the steak, then cut it with the grain into strips about ⅛ to ¼ inch thick. Combine the steak and all the remaining ingredients in a glass dish. Cover and refrigerate overnight. Place the meat on wire racks set in pans and place in the oven in a single layer. Crack open the door and bake at the lowest temperature (about 125°F) for 6 to 8 hours, or until dried.

SERVES 4 TO 6

Ronald Searle, *Right!,* from *How to Open a Bottle of Wine,* 1982

Soups and Salads

:: *Potage Saint-Germain (Fresh Pea Soup)* ::

2½ pounds English peas, shelled
  (2½ cups)
4 cups chicken broth
1 green onion, chopped, including
  green portion
2 tablespoons butter
Fresh mint or chervil sprigs for garnish

This French recipe is delicious and easy to make. It's good as a first course in spring or summer, or for lunch with a sandwich.

Cook the peas in salted boiling water until tender. Drain. In a blender, combine the peas, broth, and green onion; puree until smooth. Pour into a saucepan. Heat and add the butter. Serve immediately, garnished with mint or chervil.

SERVES 4

:: *Puree of Carrot Soup* ::

5 large carrots, peeled and sliced
1½ large onions, sliced
1 garlic clove, chopped
3 Idaho potatoes, or 2 sweet potatoes,
  peeled and sliced
4 tablespoons salted butter
2 cups water
Salt and ground white pepper to taste
2 cups milk, scalded
Minced fresh chives or parsley, or
  sautéed tiny croutons for garnish

Put all the vegetables in a heavy, medium saucepan. Add the butter, water, salt, and pepper. Bring to a boil, reduce heat, cover, and simmer until all the vegetables are very soft, about 20 minutes. Puree in a blender and return to the pan. Stir in the scalded milk. The soup may be reheated before serving, but do not let it boil. Garnish with herbs or croutons.

SERVES 4

PAGE 22 Pablo Picasso, *Still Life with Skull, Leeks, and Pitcher* (detail), March 14, 1945

:: *Asparagus, Leek, and Potato Soup* ::

4 tablespoons unsalted butter

3 large leeks, including 1 inch of green
  part, chopped

½ teaspoon dried thyme

1 bay leaf

6 cups chicken broth

1½ pounds small red potatoes, quartered

Salt and freshly ground pepper to taste

1 pound asparagus, trimmed

Melt the butter in a heavy Dutch oven over low heat. Add the leeks, thyme, and bay leaf. Cover and cook, stirring occasionally, until leeks are soft, about 10 minutes. Mix in the broth and potatoes and bring to a boil. Reduce heat, cover, and simmer until the potatoes are tender, about 12 minutes. Remove the bay leaf. Puree the mixture in a food processor or blender. Season with salt and pepper.

Steam the asparagus until crisp-tender, about 5 minutes; the cooking time will depend on the thickness of the stalks. Cut the asparagus into 1-inch pieces and add to the soup.

SERVES 12

:: *Fresh Vegetable Soup* ::

1 tablespoon butter

1 tablespoon vegetable oil

3 yellow onions, chopped

2 leeks, white part only, chopped

6 large carrots, peeled and chopped

2 zucchini chopped

2 garlic cloves

8 cups chicken broth

Leaves from 1 fresh thyme sprig, minced

Leaves from 1 fresh rosemary sprig,
  minced

Leaves from 1 fresh sage sprig, minced

Salt and freshly ground pepper to taste

2 tablespoons half-and-half

Sour cream for serving (optional)

Minced fresh herbs for garnish

A pure and healthy French soup with a lovely flavor.

Melt the butter with the oil in a soup pot. Sauté the onions and leeks over medium heat until translucent. Add the carrots and zucchini and cook for 5 minutes. Add the garlic, herbs, and broth. Bring to a boil, reduce heat, cover, and simmer for 30 minutes. Puree the mixture in batches in a food processor or blender. Return to the pot. Add the salt, pepper, and half-and half and reheat briefly. Dollop each serving with sour cream, if you like, and garnish with herbs.

SERVES 8

:: *Sinfully Healthy Soup* ::

6 cups chicken broth, plus more
  as needed
1 large Idaho potato, peeled and
  quartered
1 large yellow onion, quartered
1 garlic clove, chopped
1 bunch broccoli, chopped
½ teaspoon ground white pepper
1 bunch spinach, stemmed
2 tablespoons butter
½ pound mushrooms, stemmed
Nonfat milk as needed

Although it's perfect for people on a low-fat diet, this doesn't taste like a "healthy soup."

In a soup pot, bring the broth to a boil. Add the potato, onion, garlic, and broccoli. Reduce heat, cover, and simmer for 15 minutes, or until the potato is soft. Add the pepper and spinach; cook until the spinach wilts. Puree the vegetables and broth in a blender or food processor, in batches, if necessary. Return to the pot.

In a small skillet, melt the butter over medium heat and sauté the mushrooms until barely soft. Add to the soup. Add broth or milk as needed until the desired consistency is obtained. Reheat and serve.

SERVES 8 TO 10

:: *Melon Soup* ::

3 tablespoons sugar
1 heaping teaspoon grated, fresh ginger
½ cup dry sherry
2 large ripe cantaloupes or other melons
  (depending on season and choice),
  seeded
Mint sprigs for garnish

Serve this lovely soup for a summer lunch, with a Gewürztraminer or an Alsatian Riesling. If you like, hollow out small melons and use them to serve the soup.

Blend the sugar and ginger in a blender or food processor. Add the sherry. Scoop out the melon flesh and add to the blender or food processor in batches, if necessary. Puree until smooth. Cover and refrigerate for at least 1 hour. Garnish with mint sprigs to serve.

SERVES 8

Chelsea Botanical Dish with Melons,
ca. 1755

:: *Alsatian-Style Onion Soup* ::

2 tablespoons butter
2 tablespoons oil
3 pounds yellow onions, coarsely
  chopped
1 teaspoon salt
2 garlic cloves, minced
¼ teaspoon ground pepper
1 tablespoon Dijon mustard
1 bay leaf
2 tablespoons chicken base (optional)
6 cups chicken broth
1 cup dry white wine
Splash of brandy
8 slices dark rye bread
1 cup (4 ounces) shredded Swiss cheese
½ cup chopped fresh parsley

Melt the butter with the oil in a soup pot. Add the onions and cook, stirring occasionally, over medium heat until light brown. Add the seasonings, optional chicken base, broth, and wine. Bring to a boil, reduce heat, cover, and simmer for at least 1 hour.

To serve, preheat the oven to 400°F. Stir the brandy into the soup. Pour the soup into 8 ovenproof bowls. Float 1 slice of bread on each serving and sprinkle with 2 tablespoons cheese. Bake in the oven for 5 minutes, or until the cheese is melted. Sprinkle with the parsley.

SERVES 8

:: *Burgundy-Style Onion Soup*
Replace the white wine with dry red wine. Stir ½ cup tomato puree into soup with the seasonings.

:: *Armen's Special Soup* ::

1½ cups dried brown or green lentils
3 tablespoons olive oil
1 large onion, finely chopped
2 garlic cloves, minced
1 cup dried apricots, chopped
28 ounces canned chopped tomatoes
½ teaspoon ground cumin
½ teaspoon dried thyme
Salt and freshly ground pepper to taste
5 cups chicken broth
½ cup fresh lemon juice
Chopped fresh cilantro for garnish

Rinse and pick over the lentils. In a soup pot over medium heat, heat the oil and sauté the onion, the garlic, and the apricots until soft. Add the tomatoes and seasonings. Cover and cook for 10 to 15 minutes. Add the lentils and broth. Bring to a boil, reduce heat, cover, and simmer until the lentils are soft, about 30 minutes. If you like, puree part of the soup in a blender and return to the pot. Add the lemon juice. Taste and adjust the seasoning. Sprinkle cilantro over each bowl.

SERVES 8 TO 10

Chelsea Partridge Tureen, ca. 1754–55

:: *Red Pepper and Rice Soup* ::

2 ripe tomatoes, peeled, seeded,
   and chopped
1 tablespoon red wine vinegar
1 teaspoon packed brown sugar
4 to 5 cups beef or vegetable broth
3 red bell peppers, roasted, peeled,
   seeded, and diced
¼ cup long-grain rice
¼ teaspoon cayenne pepper or
   chili powder
2 tablespoons mild paprika
Salt and freshly ground pepper to taste

A soup from southern Spain, good in late summer when red peppers are cheap and ripe. This is nice with crusty bread and a "rough" red wine.

In a soup pot, combine the tomatoes, vinegar, and sugar and simmer until smooth and thick, about 20 minutes. Puree in a food processor and return to pot. Add the broth, peppers, rice, and seasonings. Bring to a boil, reduce heat, stir, and simmer for 15 minutes, or until rice is cooked. Taste and adjust the seasoning and add water, if necessary.

SERVES 4

:: *Capoosta (Cabbage and Neck Bone Soup)* ::

3 pounds beef neck bones, rinsed
1 teaspoon salt
Freshly ground pepper to taste
1 large onion, chopped
1 head cabbage, cored and shredded
1 tablespoon distilled white vinegar

This hearty soup is from Poland. Pork spareribs may be substituted, but they are much fattier.

In a large pot combine the bones with water to cover about halfway. Add the salt and pepper. Bring to a boil, reduce heat, add onion, cover, and simmer for 1½ hours. Remove the bones. Add the shredded cabbage and the vinegar, and cook another 20 minutes.

SERVES 6

Longton Hall Teapot and Cover,
ca. 1756

:: *Winter Vegetable and Beef Soup* ::

2 to 3 pounds beef shanks, cut crosswise

2 to 3 teaspoons salt

10 black peppercorns

1 bay leaf

2 celery stalks with green tops, sliced

1 onion, quartered

3 fresh parsley sprigs

6 cups water

28 ounces canned tomatoes, drained and chopped (reserve juice)

½ cup barley

1 cup sliced carrots

¼ teaspoon dried tarragon

¼ teaspoon curry powder

10 ounces frozen peas

½ cup sliced leek

1½ cups shredded cabbage

The curry powder is the secret ingredient that balances the broth and enriches the vegetables. You prepare the soup in advance, adding the last three ingredients just before serving. This hearty soup is perfect for a late supper, with a Gamay wine and crusty sourdough bread.

In a large pot, combine the beef shanks, 1 teaspoon of the salt, the peppercorns, bay leaf, celery, onion, parsley, and water. Bring to a boil, reduce heat, cover, and simmer for about 2 hours.

Remove the shanks and strain the broth; let cool and skim the fat from the surface. Remove the meat from the bones and cut it into 1-inch pieces. In the same pot, combine the beef broth and beef; add tomatoes and juice, the barley, carrots, tarragon, curry, and the remaining 1 to 2 teaspoons salt to your taste. Bring to a boil, reduce heat, cover, and simmer for 20 minutes. Add the peas, leek, and cabbage. Cover and simmer for 10 minutes.

SERVES 8 TO 10

James Gillray, *Temperance Enjoying a Frugal Meal*, 1792

Parting of the Loaves & Fishes

The Triumph of Benevolence

The fall of MANNA.

Table of Interest
5 p. Cent
3 Million   8,0000
3 Million 150000
3 Million 3p.C. 90000
              25000
              50000
              80000
             130000
              5000
            150000
             5000
             25p.
            150p.C.

Munificence

AQUA Regis

J.⁵ G.⁵ design.et fecit.

Pub.⁵ July 28.ᵗʰ 1792. by H. Humphry, Old Bond Street.

TEMPERANCE enjoying a Frugal Meal.

:: *Corn Soup with Egg Flowers and Pork* ::

1 tablespoon plus 1 teaspoon cornstarch

3 tablespoons water

¼ to ½ pound ground pork

1 teaspoon sugar, or to taste

½ teaspoon each salt and freshly ground
    pepper, or to taste

1 tablespoon soy sauce, or to taste

2 cups chicken broth

17 ounces canned cream-style corn

1 beaten egg

1 teaspoon Asian (toasted) sesame oil
    (optional)

In a cup, dissolve the 1 tablespoon cornstarch in the water. Set aside. Sprinkle the meat with the sugar, salt, pepper, soy sauce, and the remaining teaspoon cornstarch; stir to blend and let stand for about 15 minutes.

In a medium saucepan, bring the chicken broth to a boil, add the meat, and stir. When the soup boils again, add the corn, mix well with the meat, and simmer for about 10 minutes. (Add some water, if you like.) Bring the soup to a boil; remove from heat and drop the beaten egg slowly into the soup while stirring. Egg flowers will form. Add the cornstarch liquid to the soup mixture and mix well. Reheat if necessary. Add salt, pepper, and the sesame oil, if you like.

SERVES 4

:: *Yellow Pepper Soup with Lamb* ::

2 tablespoons butter

2 small green onions, chopped

2 tablespoons sugar

4 yellow bell peppers, seeded, deribbed,
    and finely chopped

2 tablespoons fresh lemon juice

½ cup crème fraîche

2 cups chicken broth

Pinch of saffron

Leaves from 1 fresh thyme sprig,
    chopped

Ground white pepper to taste

5 ounces loin of lamb, cut in very
    thin slices

Vessel in the Form of Chili Peppers,
South Coast Peru, 100 B.C.–A.D. 600

This soup has a gorgeous color.

In a large saucepan, melt the butter over medium heat and sauté the onions until translucent. Add the sugar and cook until the onions are slightly browned. Add the peppers, lemon juice, crème fraîche, and broth. Cover and boil for 10 minutes. Puree in a blender and strain through a sieve. Reheat and add the saffron, thyme, and pepper. Boil for 2 minutes. Divide the lamb among 6 soup bowls. Pour the soup over; the lamb will cook in the bowl.

SERVES 6

:: *Scarlet Runner Bean Soup with Lamb* ::

1 pound dried scarlet runner beans

2 tablespoons olive oil

1 large onion, chopped

½ pound lamb shoulder meat, cut
  into cubes

1 to 2 garlic cloves, minced

1 pound tomatoes, peeled, seeded, and
  chopped, or 15 ounces chunky-style
  tomato sauce

1 teaspoon chopped fresh thyme
  or oregano

1 to 2 bay leaves, crumbled

Salt and freshly ground pepper to taste

Tabasco sauce to taste

1 to 2 teaspoons sugar

2 to 4 tablespoons fresh lemon juice

3 tablespoons minced fresh mint or
  1 tablespoon dried mint

¼ to ½ cup minced fresh flat-leaf
  (Italian) parsley

Soak the beans in water to cover by 2 inches for 4 to 8 hours or overnight, then drain. In a large, heavy pot or Dutch oven over medium heat, heat the oil and sauté the onion until it begins to color. Add the lamb and garlic and sauté briefly to brown the lamb. Add the beans, tomatoes or sauce, thyme or oregano, bay leaves, and enough water to cover the beans.

Reduce heat to low and simmer slowly, uncovered, until the beans begin to soften, about 1 hour.

Add the salt, pepper, Tabasco, sugar, lemon juice, and mint. Simmer slowly, uncovered, stirring often, until the lamb and beans are very tender and the sauce is thick, about 1 to 2 hours depending on the beans. Add the parsley and simmer for 5 minutes.

This will keep for several days in the refrigerator; it reheats well.

SERVES 4

Chelsea Boar's Head Tureen, ca. 1754

:: *Fish Chowder* ::

1 pound red snapper
1 tablespoon olive oil, plus more
   as needed
1 garlic clove, put through a garlic press
1 large onion, chopped
2 celery stalks, chopped
2 cups water
1 bay leaf
28 ounces canned diced tomatoes
2 red potatoes, peeled and diced (1 cup)
½ teaspoon salt
1 tablespoon minced fresh parsley
1 teaspoon paprika
⅜ teaspoon dried thyme
½ cup dry sherry

Serve this with warm sourdough bread.

In a large skillet over medium heat, heat the oil and sauté the fish until lightly browned, 2 to 5 minutes, Turn, spread the garlic on the fish, cover, and cook for 2 to 5 minutes. Transfer the fish to a large saucepan. Add more olive oil to the frying pan, if needed, and lightly brown the onion. Add to the fish. Add the celery, water, bay leaf, tomatoes, potatoes, salt, parsley, paprika, and thyme to the saucepan. Bring to boil, reduce heat, cover, and simmer until the potatoes are just cooked, 15 to 20 minutes. Add the sherry and heat for 5 minutes.

SERVES 4

:: *Gumbo* ::

5 tablespoons butter
½ cup chopped onion
1 garlic clove, minced
3 tablespoons flour
2 cups chicken broth
16 ounces canned tomatoes, drained
   and chopped (reserve juice)
1 teaspoon salt
2 tablespoons minced fresh parsley
½ teaspoon dried thyme
2 bay leaves
2 cups fresh or frozen okra, sliced
1½ pounds medium shrimp, shelled
   and deveined
½ pound fresh lump crabmeat
1 teaspoon filé powder
3 cups cooked rice

This is an adaptation of Leontyne Price's recipe.

In a soup pot, melt 2 tablespoons of the butter over medium heat and sauté the onion and garlic for about 5 minutes. Add the remaining 3 tablespoons butter, allow to melt, and blend in the flour. Cook for 2 or 3 minutes, stirring constantly. Stir in the broth until smooth. Add the tomatoes and juice, salt, parsley, thyme, and bay leaves. Simmer, covered, for 1 hour. Add the okra, shrimp, crabmeat, and filé. Simmer for 10 minutes. Remove the bay leaves. Serve over hot rice in soup plates.

SERVES 6

:: *Creole Seafood Soup* ::

4 tablespoons butter
1 cup chopped onion
½ cup chopped green bell pepper
¼ cup flour
2 teaspoons salt
½ teaspoon freshly ground pepper
1 teaspoon dried thyme
¼ teaspoon Tabasco sauce
1 pound fresh or frozen okra, sliced
Two 28-ounce cans tomatoes, drained
   and chopped (juice reserved)
½ pound fresh lump crabmeat
½ pound medium shrimp, shelled
2 ounces scallops
2 cups milk

In a soup pot, melt the butter over medium heat and sauté the onion and green pepper until tender. Blend in the flour, salt, pepper, thyme, and Tabasco to form a smooth paste. Stir in the okra and tomatoes with juice and bring to a boil. Reduce heat, cover, and simmer until the okra is tender, about 10 minutes. Add the seafood and simmer for 4 to 5 minutes. Before serving, add the milk and heat through.

SERVES 12

PAGE 39 Samuel Marsden Brookes,
Salmon Trout and Smelt, 1873

Abraham van Beyeren, *Still Life*
(detail), 1666

:: *Cucumber-Ginger Salad* ::

½ cup rice vinegar
¼ cup water
1 tablespoon soy sauce
2 teaspoons sugar
1 tablespoon grated fresh ginger
2 cucumbers, sliced thinly on the
  diagonal
1 large carrot, peeled and sliced thinly
  on the diagonal
¼ cup sliced green onions
2 tablespoons minced fresh parsley

Combine the vinegar, water, soy sauce, sugar, and ginger in a large bowl. Add the remaining ingredients and toss well. Cover and refrigerate for 1 or 2 hours. Toss again before serving.

SERVES 6

:: *Carrot Salad Sacramento* ::

2 cups shredded carrots
⅓ cup thinly sliced celery
⅓ cup thinly sliced green onions
3 tablespoons minced fresh parsley
2 tablespoons fresh lemon juice
1 tablespoon almond or lemon oil
¾ teaspoon minced fresh basil or
  ¼ teaspoon dried basil
¼ teaspoon chili powder
⅛ teaspoon freshly ground pepper
1 garlic clove, minced
⅓ cup unblanched almonds,
  toasted and chopped
6 lettuce cups for serving
Paprika for dusting

In a large bowl, toss the carrots, celery, green onions, parsley, lemon juice, oil, basil, chili powder, pepper, and garlic together. Refrigerate for 1 to 2 hours. Just before serving, mix in the almonds. Spoon into lettuce cups and dust with paprika.

SERVES 6

Embroidered Silk Camisole (detail),
probably France, 1910–20

Salads

:: *Fuyu Persimmon Salad* ::

4 Fuyu persimmons, peeled and cut
    into ¼-inch wedges
¼ cup golden raisins
¼ cup chopped celery
2 tablespoons chopped pecans
1 to 2 tablespoons candied (crystallized)
    ginger, minced

DRESSING
2 tablespoons mayonnaise
2 tablespoons plain yogurt
1 tablespoon Major Grey's chutney, or
    ¼ teaspoon curry powder
4 large leaves of butter lettuce

*Use the firm, squat Fuyu persimmons for this salad and
the one that follows. Cut-up chicken may be added to
either salad.*

In a medium bowl, combine the persimmons, raisins,
celery, pecans, and ginger. Mix the dressing ingredients
together, add to the salad, and toss to coat. Serve on
the lettuce leaves.

SERVES 4

:: *Fuyu Persimmon Salad with Grapes* ::

4 Fuyu persimmons, peeled and cut
    into ¼-inch wedges
12 to 16 seedless green grapes, halved
    lengthwise
2 tablespoons chopped pecans or slivered
    almonds
¼ cup chopped celery
1 to 2 tablespoons candied (crystallized)
    ginger, minced
4 teaspoons dried cranberries (optional)

DRESSING
½ cup avocado oil
3 tablespoons raspberry vinegar
Salt and ground white pepper to taste
4 large leaves of butter lettuce

In a medium bowl, combine the persimmons, grapes,
nuts, celery, ginger, and optional cranberries. Whisk the
dressing ingredients together, add to the salad, and toss
to coat. Serve on the lettuce leaves.

SERVES 4

William Bailey, *Umbria Verde*, 1996

:: *Keeping Coleslaw* ::

One 6-inch head cabbage, cored
  and finely shredded
1 large onion, finely shredded
1 cup sugar

DRESSING
1 cup apple cider vinegar
1 teaspoon celery seed
1 teaspoon dry mustard
1 tablespoon salt
¾ cup vegetable oil

This slaw is called "keeping" because it will keep in the refrigerator for up to four weeks.

In a large bowl, combine the cabbage, onion, and sugar and let stand.

To make the dressing: In a small non-aluminum saucepan, combine the vinegar and celery seed and let sit for 10 minutes. Add the remaining dressing ingredients and bring to boil. Pour over the cabbage mixture and mix. Let stand in refrigerator for 4 to 6 hours before serving.

SERVES 6 TO 8

:: *Feta and Walnut Spinach Salad with Basil Dressing* ::

1 bunch spinach, washed, stemmed,
  and torn into bite-sized pieces
1 avocado, peeled, pitted, and
  thinly sliced
½ red onion, thinly sliced
½ cup crumbled feta cheese (about
  4 ounces)
½ cup coarsely chopped walnuts

BASIL DRESSING
½ cup olive oil
¼ cup red wine vinegar
3 tablespoons minced fresh basil
2 teaspoons sugar
2 garlic cloves, minced
½ teaspoon salt
¼ teaspoon freshly ground pepper

A lovely sweet and sour salad with wonderful colors and textures.

Toss the spinach, avocado, onion, feta, and walnuts together in a large bowl. Whisk the dressing ingredients together. Pour the dressing over the salad and toss.

SERVES 6

Edward Weston, *Cabbage,* 1930

:: *Green Bean Supper Salad* ::

1 pound green beans, trimmed and
    broken into sections
2 green onions, sliced
1 tomato, chopped
½ cup olive oil
¼ cup fresh lemon juice
2 tablespoons plus 1 teaspoon soy sauce
½ teaspoon ground ginger
2 tablespoons mayonnaise
2 boneless, skinless chicken breast halves,
    cooked and cut into thin strips
2 cups mixed salad greens, torn into bite-
    sized pieces
2 cups fresh bean sprouts (optional)
6 thinly sliced radishes
½ cup walnut pieces

Cook the beans in lightly salted boiling water until crisp-tender, about 5 minutes. Drain. Combine with the onions and tomato in a medium bowl.

Mix the oil, lemon juice, 2 tablespoons soy sauce, and ginger together and pour over the green bean mixture. Refrigerate for at least 1 hour, stirring occasionally. Mix the remaining teaspoon soy sauce with the mayonnaise in a small bowl, add the chicken, and mix well. Refrigerate.

Just before serving, combine the salad greens, bean sprouts, radishes, walnuts, chicken, and marinated green bean mixture in a large salad bowl. Toss to mix well.

SERVES 4

Charles Jones, *Runner Beans,* ca. 1900

:: *Tabbouleh* ::

2 cups bulgur wheat

4 cups very hot water

4 baskets cherry tomatoes, stemmed
   (3 to 4 pounds)

10 green onions

4 bunches parsley, stemmed

2 cups virgin olive oil

1½ cups fresh lemon juice

2 garlic cloves, minced

Salt to taste

1 teaspoon freshly ground pepper

This Middle Eastern salad is a great make-ahead party dish.

Soak the bulgur in the water for at least 30 minutes, so that it swells and softens. Drain. In a food processor, or with a long knife, chop separately the tomatoes, then the green onions, and the parsley. Mix the vegetables into the soaked bulgur and add the oil, lemon juice, garlic, salt, and pepper. Cover and refrigerate overnight or up to 2 days.

SERVES 6 TO 8

:: *Taco Tabbouleh* ::

1½ cups boiling water

1 cup bulgur wheat

15 ounces canned kidney beans, drained

1 bunch green onions, sliced

2 to 3 celery stalks, sliced

½ cup chopped green or red bell pepper

½ cup minced fresh parsley

1 or 2 tomatoes, chopped

DRESSING

⅓ cup white wine vinegar

⅔ cup vegetable oil

2 garlic cloves, minced

1 teaspoon salt

1 teaspoon chili powder

1½ teaspoons minced fresh oregano,
   or ½ teaspoon dried oregano

½ teaspoon ground cumin

2 or 3 tablespoons bottled salsa or canned
   diced green chilies

This can be made spicier or milder, according to individual tastes. The name refers to the fact that Mexican ingredients are added to the salad.

Pour the boiling water over the bulgur. Cover and let stand for about 1 hour. Drain if necessary. Add the vegetables. Combine all the dressing ingredients and mix with the salad.

SERVES 8 TO 10

:: *Lemon Chicken Salad* ::

2 pounds skinless, boneless chicken
  breasts
Fresh lemon juice, salt, and freshly
  ground pepper to taste

DRESSING
½ lemon with peel, cut into 6 pieces,
  deseeded
1 tablespoon minced shallot
2 tablespoons minced fresh flat-leaf
  (Italian) parsley
2 cups mayonnaise
3 tablespoons apple cider vinegar
Pinch of sugar
¼ teaspoon Tabasco sauce
Pinch of cayenne pepper
Salt and freshly ground pepper to taste

½ cup diced celery
Salad greens for serving
Toasted walnuts and sliced apples
  for garnish

Preheat the oven to 350°F. Season the chicken breast with lemon juice, salt, and pepper. Roast until the chicken is firm, about 30 to 40 minutes. Let cool and dice.

To make the dressing: In a blender or food processor, puree the lemon until smooth. Combine the pureed lemon, the shallot, parsley, mayonnaise, vinegar, sugar, Tabasco sauce, cayenne, salt, and pepper in a medium bowl and mix well.

In a large bowl, combine the celery and chicken. Add the dressing and mix well to coat. Serve on a bed of greens, topped with toasted walnuts and sliced apples.

SERVES 8

:: *Chicken Salad* ::

DRESSING

¾ cup mayonnaise

¼ cup sour cream

¼ teaspoon ground ginger, or 1 tablespoon chopped candied (crystallized)
ginger

1 teaspoon curry powder

3 green onions, minced, including
one-third of green portion

¼ teaspoon salt

1 teaspoon grated orange zest

1 tablespoon chutney, chopped

3 cups cubed cooked chicken or turkey

11 ounces canned mandarin oranges,
drained, or 1 cup seedless grapes

1 cup diced celery

½ cup sliced almonds, toasted

Mix all the dressing ingredients together. Toss the chicken or turkey, fruit, and celery with the dressing. Refrigerate for 2 hours. Sprinkle with almonds just before serving.

SERVES 3 OR 4

Roy Lichtenstein, *Sandwich and Soda*,
1964

:: *Turkey Salad with Spicy Cranberry Dressing* ::

Leaves from 1 head romaine lettuce,
  cut into 2-inch strips
Leaves from 1 head butter lettuce, torn
1 bunch watercress, stemmed
3 green onions, green portions only,
  cut into ½-inch slices
2 cups sliced cooked turkey

DRESSING
Juice of 1 lime
½ cup jellied cranberry sauce
⅓ cup mayonnaise
½ cup dried cranberries or cherries
1 teaspoon Asian (toasted) sesame oil
1 teaspoon olive oil
2 tablespoons Dijon mustard

Serve this after-Thanksgiving salad with warm sourdough bread.

Combine the lettuces, watercress, green onions and turkey in a large salad bowl.

Combine the dressing ingredients and mix thoroughly until smooth. Toss with the ingredients in the salad bowl.

SERVES 4

Virgil Solis, *Hares Roasting a Hunter*,
16th century

Salads

54

Das wir yetz hund unnd Jeger braten.

Die zal wir yetzt auch solcher mafer.

:: *Winter Bread Salad* ::

2 cups day-old bread, cut into ½-inch-
    slices
1¼ cups olive oil
⅓ cup red wine vinegar
Salt and freshly ground pepper to taste
1 small red onion, thinly sliced
¼ cup pitted Kalamata olives, cut into
    ⅛-inch slices
2 ounces ricotta salata or any hard
    sheep cheese, crumbled
1 head radicchio, cored and thinly sliced
Leaves from 2 heads frisée
1 bunch arugula

Sourdough or walnut bread are good in this salad, but any hearty bread will do.

Preheat the oven to 350°F. Put the bread in a large bowl and toss with ¼ cup of the olive oil. Spread in one layer in a baking dish and toast in the oven for about 10 minutes.

In a medium bowl, whisk the vinegar, salt, pepper, and remaining 1 cup olive oil together.

Put the toasted bread in a large bowl and toss with half of the dressing. Let stand for 30 minutes. Add all the remaining ingredients and the remaining dressing. Toss to coat, and serve.

SERVES 6 TO 8

:: *Garbanzo Bean and Salami Salad* ::

2 tablespoons extra virgin olive oil

1 tablespoon balsamic vinegar

1 to 2 tablespoons fresh lemon juice

½ garlic clove, minced

¼ cup Italian salad dressing

1 teaspoon minced fresh oregano
  or thyme

1 to 2 teaspoons sugar

Salt and freshly ground pepper to taste

4 cups cooked garbanzo beans, drained
  and rinsed

¼ cup chopped red onion

8 slices salami, cut into ½-inch squares

2 Roma (plum) tomatoes, seeded
  and chopped

2 tablespoons minced fresh mint

4 to 6 tablespoons minced flat-leaf
  (Italian) parsley

Lettuce leaves for serving

In a medium bowl, beat the oil, vinegar, lemon juice, garlic, salad dressing, herb, sugar, salt, and pepper together with a fork. Add the beans and stir well. The salad may be made ahead to this point and refrigerated until ready to serve. Before serving, add the onion, salami, tomatoes, mint, and parsley and mix well. Serve on plates lined with lettuce leaves.

SERVES 4 AS A MAIN COURSE OR 8 AS AN APPETIZER

Storage Basket, Yokuts, California,
early 20th century

Vegetables and Grains

:: *Asparagus Soufflé* ::

½ pound fresh asparagus, trimmed
1½ tablespoons butter
1½ tablespoons flour
½ cup milk
¼ teaspoon salt
Dash of ground nutmeg
2 eggs, separated

A soufflé for two—hard to find.

Preheat the oven to 400°F. Cook the asparagus in salted boiling water until crisp-tender, about 4 minutes. Drain, reserving 2 tablespoons liquid. Cut the asparagus into 1-inch lengths. Reserve the tips and place the remainder in a buttered 3-cup baking dish or soufflé dish.

In a small, heavy saucepan, melt the butter over medium heat and mix in the flour. Stir until the mixture boils and thickens. Stir in the milk, salt, and nutmeg. Let cool slightly, then whisk in the egg yolks. In a large bowl, beat the egg whites until stiff, glossy peaks form. Fold into the milk mixture. Spoon over the asparagus on the baking dish. Arrange the asparagus tips on top. Bake for 18 minutes, or until puffed and set in the center.

SERVES 2

:: *Braised Red Cabbage with Apples* ::

1 head red cabbage, cored and shredded
¼ cup long-grain rice
2 unpeeled tart, cooking apples, cored
  and diced
½ teaspoon salt
1 tablespoon butter
⅓ cup sugar
¼ cup apple cider vinegar
½ cup water

This fragrant side dish is even better when made one day ahead and reheated.

In a medium non-aluminum saucepan, combine all the ingredients, bring to a boil, cover and simmer for 45 minutes. Add more water, if needed, while cooking. Serve immediately, or let cool, cover, and refrigerate overnight. Reheat to serve.

SERVES 8

PAGE 58 Thomas Waterman Wood,
Market Woman, 1858

:: *Paprika Cauliflower and Noodles* ::

3 tablespoons butter

1¼ cups chopped onions

2 tablespoons flour

1¼ teaspoons prepared horseradish

1 cup sour cream

1 cup plain yogurt

2 teaspoons paprika, plus more
 for garnish

½ teaspoon salt

Freshly ground pepper to taste

1 cauliflower, broken into florets

12 ounces dried egg noodles

2 tablespoons poppy seeds

2 tablespoons minced fresh dill or
 2 teaspoons dried dill

2 tablespoons minced fresh chives

A savory and hearty vegetarian main dish.

In a medium, heavy saucepan, melt 1½ tablespoons of the butter over medium heat and sauté the onions until glazed and softened. Add the flour, mix well, and cook the mixture for 2 minutes, stirring constantly. Using a slotted spoon, stir in the horseradish, sour cream, and yogurt. Cook, stirring constantly, for 5 minutes. Add the 2 teaspoons paprika, the salt, and pepper. Set aside and keep warm.

Steam the cauliflower until tender, then add to the sauce. Meanwhile, in a large pot of salted boiling water, cook the noodles until al dente. Drain.

Put the noodles in a large serving casserole and toss them with the poppy seeds and remaining 1½ tablespoons butter. Ladle the hot sauce over the hot noodles. Top with the dill and chives and sprinkle with paprika.

SERVES 4 AS A SIDE DISH OR 2 AS A MAIN DISH

:: *Eggplant Parmigiana* ::

TOMATO SAUCE

2 tablespoons olive oil

3 to 4 cups chopped onions

5 cups tomatoes, peeled, seeded, and
cut into ⅜-inch strips

2 large garlic cloves, finely minced
or pressed

1 tablespoon chopped fresh basil

Salt and freshly ground pepper to taste

¼ cup cornmeal (preferably
stone ground)

2 eggs, beaten

4 tablespoons olive oil

2 eggplants, cut into ⅜-inch
crosswise slices

¾ cup (3 ounces) finely grated domestic
Romano cheese

¾ cup (3 ounces) shredded Gruyère
cheese

6 teaspoons minced fresh basil

6 teaspoons minced fresh parsley

2 tablespoons unsalted butter or
margarine

The tomato sauce may be prepared one day ahead.

To make the tomato sauce: In a large skillet over medium heat, heat the olive oil and sauté the onions until translucent. Add the tomatoes, garlic, basil, and salt, and pepper. Cover and cook for 5 minutes, or until the tomatoes have begun to render their juice. Uncover, stir, and simmer until the juice has almost entirely evaporated, 20 to 30 minutes. Use immediately, or let cool, cover, and refrigerate overnight. Reheat before assembling dish.

Preheat the oven to 350°F. Add the cornmeal to the eggs and stir until blended. In a large nonstick skillet over medium heat, heat 2 tablespoons of the oil. Dip half the eggplant slices in the batter and fry in batches until lightly browned on both sides. Repeat with the remaining 2 tablespoons olive oil and eggplant.

Preheat an 11-inch oval gratin dish or 12-inch enameled cast-iron casserole. Spread one-third of the tomato sauce in the dish. Combine the 2 cheeses and toss to mix. Sprinkle with one-third of the cheese mixture and 2 teaspoons *each* basil and parsley. Top with half of the eggplant slices. Pour half the remaining tomato sauce over the eggplant and sprinkle with half the remaining cheese mixture and half the remaining basil and parsley. Top with the remaining eggplant slices. Spread the remaining tomato sauce over the eggplant and sprinkle with the remaining basil, parsley, and cheese mixture. Dot with butter or margarine and bake for 30 to 40 minutes. Let stand for 4 to 5 minutes before serving.

SERVES 8 AS AN APPETIZER, 4 AS A MAIN DISH

Mark Adams, *Eggplant,* 1978

:: Basque Potatoes ::

6 tablespoons unsalted butter
3 tablespoons olive oil
3 large garlic cloves, crushed
½ cup minced fresh parsley
1½ teaspoons minced fresh thyme,
 or ½ teaspoon dried thyme
4 teaspoons minced fresh rosemary,
 or 1½ teaspoons dried rosemary
1½ teaspoons paprika
Dash of cayenne pepper
3 pounds small new white or red
 potatoes, scrubbed and patted dry
½ teaspoon salt
¼ teaspoon freshly ground pepper

These go well with roasts and grilled meat or fish.

Preheat the oven to 375°F. In a large roasting pan, melt the butter with the oil over medium heat. Add the garlic, parsley, thyme, rosemary, paprika, and cayenne. Add the potatoes and roll them in the seasoned butter to coat well. Bake, basting the potatoes occasionally with the butter for about 40 minutes, or until the potatoes are tender. Season with salt and pepper.

SERVES 8 TO 10

:: Gomae (Spinach with Sesame Dressing) ::

1 bunch spinach, washed and stemmed
2 tablespoons sesame seeds
1 tablespoon sugar
1½ tablespoons soy sauce

This is a great way to serve spinach. Steamed green beans, broccoli, or asparagus may be substituted.

Cook the spinach in salted boiling water for 1 to 2 minutes. Drain well. Rinse in cold water and set aside. Heat a small, heavy saucepan over medium heat. Add the sesame seeds, cover, and shake the pan until the seeds pop. Grind the sesame seeds in a mortar, or in a hand-held grinder. Add the sugar and soy sauce to the sesame seeds and mix well. Chop the spinach into 1 to 1½-inch pieces. Squeeze the excess water from the spinach and mix with the sesame dressing.

SERVES 4

Lion-Shaped Rhyton (Libation Vessel),
Anatolian, ca. 1860–1780 B.C.

:: *Tomatoes Provençale* ::

5 Roma (plum) tomatoes, cut into
  ½-inch-thick slices
¼ cup olive oil
3 garlic cloves, minced
3 tablespoons fresh basil, finely chopped
Salt and freshly ground pepper to taste

Serve on crostini as an appetizer, as a side dish for fish, or toss with your favorite pasta.

Preheat oven to 350°F. Line a jelly roll pan with parchment paper. Place the tomato slices in the pan in one layer. Brush the tomato slices liberally on both sides with the olive oil. Sprinkle with the garlic, basil, salt, and pepper. Bake for 20 minutes.

SERVES 8

:: *Zucchini à la Grecque* ::

¼ cup red wine vinegar
1 to 2 garlic cloves, pressed and minced
Salt and freshly ground pepper to taste
2 pounds zucchini, cut into ¼-inch-thick
  lengthwise slices
2 tablespoons olive oil
½ cup chopped walnuts

This dish can be made several hours ahead of serving, but it should be not refrigerated.

Mix the vinegar and garlic in a small cup and set aside. Salt and pepper the zucchini. In a large skillet over medium heat, heat the oil and fry the zucchini until browned on each side. Drain on paper towels. Make 1 layer of zucchini on a platter. Sprinkle the vinegar mixture lightly over the zucchini and sprinkle with a light layer of walnuts. Repeat the layering to use the remaining ingredients.

SERVES 6 TO 8

:: *Autumn Vegetable Ragout* ::

1 large eggplant, peeled and sliced
   ¼-inch thick
Salt for sprinkling
4 tablespoons olive oil
2 large onions, chopped
6 garlic cloves, minced
2 teaspoons minced fresh ginger
1½ cups fresh bread crumbs
3 zucchini, sliced ¼-inch thick
3 yellow crookneck squash, sliced
   ¼-inch thick
5 tomatoes, sliced ¼-inch thick, or 28
   ounces canned tomatoes, drained and
   chopped
Salt and freshly ground pepper to taste
1 cup minced fresh parsley
1 cup (4 ounces) grated Parmesan cheese

A versatile make-ahead dish that is good served hot or at room temperature for an informal lunch. It is better made a day in advance and reheated so the flavors intensify and blend. Make this into a one-dish meal by adding eight Italian sausages that have been browned and cut into one-inch pieces.

Sprinkle the eggplant with salt and let drain on paper towels for 20 minutes. Blot dry and cut into 1-inch cubes.

Preheat the oven to 350°F. Lightly grease a 12-inch round or oval gratin dish.

In a large skillet over medium heat, heat 2 table-spoons of the oil and sauté the onions until limp. Add the garlic and ginger. Remove from heat. Stir in the bread crumbs. Sprinkle half the mixture over the bottom of the prepared dish. Arrange the vegetables in layers over the onion mixture. Drizzle with the remaining 2 tablespoons oil. Top with the remaining onion mixture.

Cover tightly with aluminum foil and bake for 30 minutes. Add the salt and pepper. Combine the parsley and Parmesan cheese and sprinkle over the top. Return, uncovered, to the oven and bake until cheese melts.

SERVES 4

:: *Biscuit Pie* ::

DOUGH

2½ cups self-rising flour

½ cup (1 stick) cold butter, cut into
    small pieces

1½ tablespoons minced fresh basil or
    1½ teaspoons dried basil

¾ cup half-and-half

FILLING

1½ pounds ripe tomatoes cut into
    ½-inch-thick slices

1 cup (4 ounces) shredded Monterey
    jack cheese

¼ cup (1 ounce) grated Parmesan cheese

½ red bell pepper, seeded, deribbed,
    and sliced

½ cup chopped green onions

¼ cup virgin olive oil

A tomato and cheese pie that's great for picnics. This is adapted from a recipe by Harvey Steiman, published in the San Francisco Chronicle *in 1992.*

To make the dough: Preheat the oven to 400°F. Butter a 9-inch pie pan. Combine the flour, butter, and basil in a food processor. Process for 10 to 15 seconds, then add the half-and-half and process until a ball begins to form. To make by hand, cut the butter into the flour with a pastry cutter or 2 knives until the mixture resembles coarse crumbs. Stir in the half-and-half with a fork to moisten the dry mixture. Form into a ball with your hands. Knead the dough on lightly floured surface a few times. Divide the dough into 2 pieces, one slightly larger than the other. Roll out the larger piece to an 11-inch diameter. Fit into the pan.

To make the filling: Place the tomatoes in the crust. Sprinkle with the cheese, red pepper, and onions and drizzle with the oil. Roll out the remaining dough to a thickness of ⅛ inch and place over the pie. Trim the edges of the 2 pieces of pastry, fold them under, and flute. Cut decorative vents in the top pastry. Bake for about 35 minutes, or until well browned. Serve at room temperature.

SERVES 4 TO 6

Jerome Thompson, *Recreation* (detail),
1857

:: *Fresh Corn Pudding* ::

12 medium-sized ears fresh corn, shucked

About ⅔ cup milk or cream as needed for curdled cream consistency (more is needed for old corn and winter corn)

3 to 5 tablespoons butter

Salt and freshly ground pepper to taste

1 to 2 tablespoons sugar, if the corn is not fresh from the garden

Fresh corn is the key to this simple pudding.

Preheat the oven to 375°F. Using a corn scraper (available in some supermarkets and kitchenware stores) or a grater, scrape the juice from the kernels into a buttered baking dish. Add enough milk or cream to make the corn look like thick curdled cream. Add the salt, pepper, and optional sugar. Dot with butter. Bake for 45 minutes to 1 hour, or until pudding is firm.

SERVES 4

:: *Brown Rice with Nuts and Dried Fruit* ::

3 tablespoons vegetable oil

1 small onion, chopped

½ cup chopped dried apricots

½ cup chopped dried cranberries

⅔ cup chopped mixed nuts

⅓ cup sesame seeds

¼ to ½ teaspoon ground cloves

½ teaspoon salt

3 cups cooked brown rice

4 tablespoons butter, melted

This is great with chicken or fish.

Preheat the oven to 350°F. Butter a 6-cup baking dish.

In a large skillet over medium heat, heat the oil and sauté the onion, fruit, nuts, and sesame seeds until the onion is translucent, about 5 minutes. Add the cloves and salt to the onion mixture and stir. Add the rice and mix well. Put the rice in the prepared dish and pour the melted butter over all. Bake for 15 to 20 minutes, or until heated through. Serve immediately.

SERVES 4

Bowls (Umeke), Hawaiian Islands, 18th–19th century

:: *Baked Rice with Herbs* ::

3 tablespoons olive oil
½ cup chopped onion
½ cup chopped celery
½ cup chopped mushrooms
¼ cup chopped fresh parsley
1 garlic clove, minced
1½ cups long-grain rice
2 cups chicken broth
1 cup dry white wine
Pinch *each* of dried thyme and rosemary
Salt and freshly ground pepper to taste

Preheat the oven to 350°F. In a heavy, flameproof 8-cup casserole, heat the oil over medium-low heat and sauté the onion, celery, mushrooms, parsley, and garlic for 5 minutes. Add the rice and sauté for 2 to 3 minutes. Add the broth, wine, thyme, rosemary, salt, and pepper. Bring to a boil, cover, place in the oven, and bake for 30 minutes. Uncover and stir gently with a fork; then cover and continue baking for about 10 minutes, or until tender.

SERVES 6 TO 8

:: *Gourmet Polenta* ::

3 cups water
½ cup (1 stick) unsalted butter
1 teaspoon salt, or to taste
Freshly ground pepper to taste
¾ cup polenta
1 to 1½ teaspoons minced garlic sautéed
  in a little butter
½ cup chopped fresh basil
1 to 1½ cups ricotta cheese
1 tablespoon minced fresh oregano
  (optional)
Small handful grated Italian Parmesan
  cheese

Bring the water and butter to a boil in a large, heavy saucepan. Add the salt and pepper. With a wooden spoon, slowly stir in the polenta until a smooth mixture forms. Reduce heat and simmer, stirring frequently, for 20 to 25 minutes, or until thickened. Stir in the remaining ingredients.

SERVES 8 TO 10 GENEROUSLY

Bowl in the Form of a Squash Supported by Standing Men, Colima, Mexico, 200 B.C.–A.D. 300

:: *Vegetarian Black Bean Chili* ::

4 to 5 cups dried black beans
2½ tablespoons cumin seed
2½ tablespoons dried oregano
½ cup olive oil
2 to 3 large yellow onions, chopped
2 pounds green bell peppers, seeded, deribbed, and chopped
5 to 8 celery stalks, chopped (optional)
3 to 5 garlic cloves, minced (optional)
1½ teaspoons cayenne pepper
1½ tablespoons paprika
¼ cup minced fresh cilantro, plus 10 to 20 fresh cilantro sprigs
1 teaspoon salt
3 cups canned whole tomatoes, drained and crushed (juice reserved)
Tomato paste to taste (optional)
2 to 3 jalapeño chilies, seeded and minced
¾ to 1 pound shredded Monterey jack or Cheddar cheese
1 cup sour cream
1½ cups finely chopped green onions

This freezes nicely and is great with polenta and salad.

Rinse and pick over the beans. Soak overnight in water to cover by 2 inches. Drain. In a soup pot, combine the beans with water to cover by 2 inches. Bring to a boil, reduce heat, cover, and cook until tender, about 1 hour. Drain, reserving 2 cups liquid.

In a small dry skillet, stir the cumin and oregano over medium heat until fragrant. Set aside.

In a large, heavy pot or Dutch oven over medium heat, heat the oil and sauté the onions, peppers, celery, and garlic with the cumin, oregano, cayenne, paprika, minced cilantro, and salt for 10 to 15 minutes, or until the onions are soft. Add the tomatoes and juice, optional tomato paste, and chilies. Add the beans and stir. Cook for 15 to 30 minutes. Divide the cheese among the bowls. Top with chili, cilantro sprigs, sour cream, and green onions.

SERVES 8 TO 10

Glen Baxter, *The Fourth Time*, 1984

IT WAS THE FOURTH TIME THAT DADDY HAD
FALLEN FOR THE EXPLODING FORK ROUTINE...

:: *Pasta with Vodka* ::

5 tablespoons butter

⅔ cup vodka

¼ teaspoon red pepper flakes or more
    to taste

16 ounces canned Italian (plum)
    tomatoes, drained and pureed in
    a blender or food processor

¾ cup heavy cream

½ teaspoon salt

1 pound penne or other tubular pasta

¾ cup (3 ounces) grated Parmesan cheese

1 tablespoon minced fresh parsley

This spectacular pasta dish is from the Vecchia Bettola Trattoria in Florence, Italy. It can be assembled from start to finish in about 15 minutes.

Melt the butter in a large skillet over medium heat. Add the vodka and pepper flakes and simmer for 2 minutes. Add the pureed tomatoes and the cream; simmer for 5 minutes. Add the salt. Meanwhile, in a large pot of salted boiling water, cook the pasta until al dente (cooked through, but chewy), about 10 minutes. Drain well in a colander. Pour the pasta into the skillet with the hot sauce. Reduce heat to low, add the cheese, and mix thoroughly. Pour into heated bowls and sprinkle each serving with a little parsley. Serve at once.

SERVES 4 TO 6

Wesley Chamberlin, *Seagram's,* 1974

Meat, Poultry, Fish, and Seafood

:: Chinkiang Spareribs ::

1 tablespoon Shaoxing rice wine or
   dry sherry
2 tablespoons sugar
3 tablespoons Gold Plum Chinkiang
   vinegar (found in Asian markets)
2 tablespoons *each* dark and light
   soy sauce
5 tablespoons water
2 tablespoons peanut oil
3 to 4 thin slices fresh ginger
3 green onions
1½ pounds pork spareribs

Black vinegar from Zhejiang, China, adds a smoky flavor to these ribs. Serve them with steamed rice.

In a small bowl, mix the wine, sugar, vinegar, soy sauce, and water together.

   In a wok or large skillet over high heat, heat the oil. Stir in the ginger and green onions. Add the wine mixture, stir, and immediately add the spareribs. Stir to coat well. Cover and bring to a boil, then reduce heat and simmer until the liquid is reduced to a thick sauce and the ribs are tender, about 30 minutes.

SERVES 4 TO 6

:: Oven-Baked Chinese Pork Chops ::

1 egg
3 tablespoons soy sauce
1 tablespoon dry sherry
⅛ teaspoon ground ginger
1 garlic clove, minced
¼ cup dried bread crumbs
4 loin pork chops, 1 inch thick,
   trimmed of fat

This delicious low-fat dish is excellent with sweet potatoes and a green vegetable.

Preheat the oven to 350°F. Coat a nonstick baking pan with vegetable-oil cooking spray.

   In a shallow bowl, beat together all the ingredients except the chops until blended. Dip each chop in the mixture, pressing down so the crumbs adhere on both sides. Arrange the chops in a single layer in the pan. Bake for 30 minutes. Turn and bake 20 to 30 minutes longer, or until tender.

SERVES 4

PAGE 78 Tapestry, *The Last Supper* (detail), from *Scenes from the Life of Christ*, Brussels, ca. 1510

Arnold Genthe, *The Vegetable Peddler*, ca. 1896

:: *Roast Pork Tenderloin* ::

¼ cup soy sauce
¼ cup bourbon
2½ tablespoons packed brown sugar
3 pounds center-cut pork tenderloin

Serve with warm homemade applesauce.

Mix the soy sauce, bourbon, and brown sugar in a small bowl. Place the pork in a glass baking dish. Pour the soy sauce mixture over the pork. Cover and refrigerate for at least 3 hours, turning every hour.

Preheat the oven to 325°F. Remove the pork from the marinade and place on a rack in a shallow roasting pan. Bake for 1 hour, basting every 15 minutes.

SERVES 6

Grant Wood, *Dinner for Threshers,* 1934

:: *Easy Lamb Shanks* ::

4 lamb shanks
Garlic salt to taste
Salt and paprika to taste
4 onions, chopped
1 cup dry white wine, vermouth, or
  chicken broth

A simple way to cook lamb shanks. Serve with rice, or add new potatoes and carrots.

Preheat the broiler. Season the meat well with the garlic salt, salt, and paprika. Brown the shanks (on aluminum foil) under the broiler. Transfer to a Dutch oven or baking dish and add the onions and wine or broth. Set the oven temperature at 325°F. Cover and bake for 1 hour, then lower the temperature to 275°F and bake for 1½ hours, or until very tender.

SERVES 4

Meat

:: *Moussaka with Artichokes* ::

6 large artichokes

MEAT SAUCE
1½ pounds ground lamb
1 onion, finely chopped
1 cup tomato sauce
1 tablespoon tomato paste
1 cup dry red wine
⅛ teaspoon ground cinnamon
Salt and freshly ground pepper to taste

WHITE SAUCE
4 tablespoons butter
¼ cup flour
1½ cups milk, heated
2 eggs, beaten
Ground nutmeg, salt, and freshly ground
   pepper to taste

1 cup minced fresh parsley
1 tablespoon grated Parmesan cheese

*This moussaka is made with artichokes in place of eggplant.
You can assemble it on one day and bake it the next.*

Cook the artichokes in salted boiling water until tender,
about 1 hour. Drain upside down. Remove the leaves,
scraping off the meat at the base. Remove and chop the
stems. Dig out the chokes with a teaspoon and discard
them. Cut each heart into quarters. Set aside.

To make the meat sauce: In a large, heavy skillet, cook the
lamb and onion over medium heat, stirring frequently,
until the meat is browned. Stir in the tomato sauce and
paste, wine, cinnamon, salt, and pepper. Cook until
thickened. Set aside.

Preheat the oven to 350°F.

To make the white sauce: In a medium saucepan, melt the
butter over low heat. Stir in the flour and cook, stirring,
for 2 or 3 minutes. Gradually whisk in the hot milk and
cook, stirring frequently, until thickened. Remove from
heat and let cool slightly. Stir in the beaten eggs and
seasonings.

In an 8 × 12-inch glass baking dish, make a layer of half
the artichokes topped with half the parsley, and then
with half the meat sauce. Repeat. Cover with the white
sauce and sprinkle with Parmesan. Bake for 1 hour, or
until bubbling and browned.

SERVES 8

Eugène Feuillatre, *Enameled Silver
Vase with Base in the Form of an
Artichoke*, ca. 1900

:: *Le Lapin Agile au Chocolat* ::

One 3- to 5-pound rabbit, cut up
Salt and freshly ground pepper to taste
½ cup yellow cornmeal
½ cup whole wheat flour
2 tablespoons butter
2 tablespoons light olive oil
2½ tablespoons all-purpose flour
1½ cups chicken broth
1 ounce unsweetened chocolate, melted
¼ teaspoon ground cinnamon
1 teaspoon ground mace
½ cup finely chopped onion
1 cup grated carrot
½ cup raisins
12 pitted prunes
Minced fresh parsley and whole almonds
   for garnish

The name for this West Indian recipe for rabbit baked in a spicy dark sauce may come from a famous Parisian cabaret, Au Lapin Agile.

Preheat the oven to 325°F. Season the rabbit with salt and pepper. Dredge with the cornmeal and whole wheat flour. Melt the butter with the olive oil in a large skillet over medium heat. Add the rabbit and brown on both sides. Transfer the rabbit to an ovenproof dish.

Add the all-purpose flour to the pan drippings and stir over medium heat until lightly browned. Gradually stir in the broth and cook, stirring frequently, until thickened. Stir in the chocolate, cinnamon, and mace. Add salt and pepper to taste, if needed. Stir in the onion, carrot, raisins, and prunes. Pour over the rabbit, cover, and bake for 45 minutes, or until tender. Garnish with parsley and almonds.

SERVES 6 TO 8

Tapestry, *Rabbit-Hunting with Ferrets* (detail), probably Tournai, 1460–70

:: *Beef and Asparagus with Black Bean Sauce* ::

1 teaspoon soy sauce

1 teaspoon sugar

1 teaspoon cornstarch

1 teaspoon Shaoxing rice wine or dry
   sherry (optional)

1 tablespoon Chinese black bean sauce
   (available in Asian markets)

2 garlic cloves, minced

½ pound flank steak, thinly sliced

2 tablespoons peanut oil

1 pound asparagus, trimmed and cut into
   2-inch diagonal slices

Salt to taste

Steamed rice for serving

In a small bowl, stir the soy sauce, sugar, cornstarch, and wine together; set aside. Mix the black bean sauce and garlic together; set aside. Put the meat in a bowl and stir in half of the soy sauce mixture. Let sit at room temperature for 15 minutes.

In a wok or large skillet over high heat, heat 1 tablespoon of the oil. Add the asparagus and stir-fry until crisp-tender, 2 to 3 minutes. Season with salt and set aside. Reheat pan and add the remaining 1 tablespoon oil. Add the bean sauce mixture and stir. Add the meat and stir-fry just until it loses its pink color. Stir in the asparagus and the remaining soy sauce mixture. Serve at once over rice.

SERVES 4

:: *Tamarind-Coconut Beef* ::

1 cup unsweetened grated coconut

3 garlic cloves, thinly sliced

1-inch piece ginger, cut into thin slices

1 stalk lemongrass, trimmed to 6 inches,
   peeled of outer leaves, and thinly sliced

2 tablespoons minced shallots

1 teaspoon ground turmeric

1 teaspoon ground cumin

2 tablespoons peanut oil

3 to 4 pounds boneless beef chuck roast
   or round steak, cut into 2-inch cubes,
   then ¼-inch thick slices

4 cups coconut milk

2 tablespoons tamarind paste

3 to 4 fresh or dried kaffir lime leaves, cut
   into thin strips

Salt to taste

Look for the lemongrass, tamarind paste, coconut milk, and lime leaves in Southeast Asian markets. Serve this with steamed rice and Indonesian chili paste.

Stir the coconut in a dry skillet over low heat until toasted; set aside. Combine the garlic, ginger, lemongrass, shallots, turmeric, and cumin in a small food processor or grinder and process to a paste.

In a large, heavy pot or Dutch oven over medium heat, heat the peanut oil and fry the paste for a few minutes. Add the beef and cook, stirring frequently, for 5 to 10 minutes. Add the coconut milk, tamarind paste, and lime leaves; reduce heat and cook for 30 minutes, or until thickened. Add the salt.

SERVES 4

Meat

:: *Handi Kabob* ::

MARINADE
⅓ cup plain yogurt
½ teaspoon ground ginger
½ teaspoon minced garlic
½ teaspoon ground pepper
2 bay leaves
¼ teaspoon ground cloves
¼ teaspoon ground cinnamon
½ teaspoon salt

2 pounds beef round roast
1 tablespoon vegetable oil
2 tablespoons finely chopped onions

This dish is famous in Pakistan. Handi *is the name of the metal container in which it is traditionally cooked.*

Blend all the marinade ingredients together. Prick the meat all over with a fork, cut it into 1½-inch cubes, and place in a glass baking dish. Brush meat with the marinade on all sides, cover, and refrigerate overnight.

In a deep, heavy pot over medium heat, heat the oil and brown the onions. Add the meat, cover, and cook over low heat for about 1 hour, or until tender. Add a little water if necessary while cooking. Serve with rice or naan bread and a salad of onions and tomatoes.

SERVES 4

:: *Kål Dolmar* ::

1 large head cabbage, cored
1 pound ground beef
1 cup cooked rice
1 teaspoon minced fresh parsley
1 egg
⅓ cup milk
¼ cup finely chopped onion
1 teaspoon salt
Pinch of ground pepper
2 tablespoons oil
2 tablespoons packed brown sugar
2 tablespoons apple cider vinegar
½ cup water
1 bay leaf
4 whole cloves

The Swedish version of Middle Eastern stuffed grape leaves, dolmar *are stuffed cabbage leaves. They are usually served with potatoes and* limpa, *the Swedish rye bread.*

In a large pot of salted boiling water, cook the cabbage, covered, for 4 or 5 minutes. Drain well and let cool a bit. Remove 12 of the outer leaves and set aside.

In a medium bowl, combine the meat, rice, parsley, egg, milk, onion, salt, and pepper. Mix until well blended. Divide the mixture among the leaves, placing a mound at the stem end of each leaf. Roll up each leaf and fasten with a toothpick.

In a large non-aluminum skillet over medium heat, heat the oil and brown the bundles on both sides. Combine all the remaining ingredients and pour over the bundles. Lower heat, cover, and simmer for 1 hour.

MAKES 12 DOLMAR; SERVES 6

Meat

:: *Oxtail Stew* ::

2 oxtails, about 2 inches thick
Salt and freshly ground pepper to taste
8 tablespoons butter
2 carrots, peeled and quartered
4 medium to large onions, quartered
⅓ cup brandy
¼ cup flour
¾ bottle good dry red wine, such as
  Syrah or Mourvèdre
Bouquet garni: bay leaf, thyme, and
  parsley, tied in a cheesecloth bag
3 or 4 garlic cloves
3 tablespoons oil
1 teaspoon fresh lemon juice
1 to 2 pounds mushrooms
Buttered fresh pasta for serving

Make sure the oxtails are fresh and not fatty for this delicious dish.

Preheat the oven to 300°F. Season the oxtails with salt and pepper. In a heavy flameproof casserole or Dutch oven, melt 4 tablespoons of the butter over medium heat and cook the carrots and onions, stirring frequently, until lightly browned. Remove from the pan. Add the oxtails and cook, stirring frequently for 10 to 15 minutes, or until they have browned evenly. Return the vegetables to the pan and mix them with the oxtails. Pour the brandy into the pan, let it heat, avert your face, and light the brandy with a long-handled match. Stir until the flames subside. Add the flour and stir for about 5 minutes to cook the flour evenly and completely. Add the red wine, bouquet garni, and garlic cloves. Stir constantly until the liquid comes to a boil.

Cover and braise in the oven for 2 hours. Transfer the meat to a plate, leaving the oven on. Strain the basting liquid into another pan and let cool. Discard the bouquet garni and the aromatic vegetables. Return the meat to the braising pan.

In a medium or large skillet, melt the remaining 4 tablespoons butter with the oil over medium heat. Add the lemon juice and mushrooms and cook until the mushrooms release their liquid. Add the mushrooms to the meat.

Degrease the braising liquid and simmer it for about 15 minutes, or until reduced by a quarter. Pour the liquid over the meat and mushrooms. Cover and bake for about 1½ hours, or until the meat is very tender, basting the meat several times with the cooking juices. Serve the oxtails straight from the pan, with pasta.

SERVES 4

Porringer and Stand, London, 1662

:: *Flank Steak, California Style* ::

2 tablespoons soy sauce
¼ cup fresh lime juice
¼ cup beer
2 tablespoons olive oil
2 garlic cloves, pressed
2 jalapeño chilies, seeded and minced
½ teaspoon freshly ground pepper
½ teaspoon salt
2 pounds flank steak

The marinated steak can also be grilled. The leftovers are great for fajitas.

In a blender, combine and puree all the ingredients except the flank steak. Cut 4 shallow slashes across the grain on each side of the flank steak. Place in a glass dish and pour in the marinade, rubbing the garlic into the slashes. Cover and refrigerate for at least 2 hours, but preferably overnight.

Remove the steak from the refrigerator 30 minutes before cooking. Preheat the broiler. Place the steak on a broiler pan (reserve the marinade) about 4 inches from the heat and cook for about 6 minutes per side for rare, 8 minutes for medium, and 10 minutes for well done. The length of time depends on the thickness of the steak. Don't overcook the meat.

Meanwhile, boil the marinade in a small saucepan to reduce it. Slice the steak on the diagonal and serve the reduced marinade alongside.

SERVES 6

:: Traditional Jewish Brisket ::

5 large onions, sliced
4 pounds beef brisket
3 garlic cloves, minced
1 bottle chili sauce (not Mexican)

This Jewish family recipe won first prize at a Catholic school cookoff! If you keep your mouth closed when peeling and slicing the onion, you will have no tears.

Preheat the oven to 275°F. Layer half the onions in a roasting pan. Place the brisket on top of the onions. Cover with the remaining onions and the garlic. Bake uncovered for 1 hour. Pour the chili sauce over the meat, cover, and bake for 2½ to 3 hours, or until meat is fork-tender. Let cool. Skim the fat from the gravy. Slice the meat across the grain and return to the gravy. Reheat and serve.

SERVES 8 TO 10

:: Beef Sirloin with Wild Mushrooms and Zinfandel Sauce ::

3 tablespoons flour
¼ teaspoon *each* salt and ground pepper
1 pound beef sirloin, cut into cubes
3 tablespoons butter
1 tablespoon olive oil
1 small onion, halved and cut into
  thin vertical slices
8 new potatoes, blanched
1 garlic clove, minced
1 teaspoon minced fresh thyme
1 zucchini, halved and cut into
  wedges
2 tomatoes, quartered
4 ounces wild mushrooms, thickly sliced
½ cup good quality Zinfandel wine

This dish goes well with roasted new potatoes, rice, or pasta.

Mix the flour, salt, and pepper together. Add the meat and toss to coat it evenly. In a large skillet, melt 1 tablespoon of the butter with the olive oil and heat to almost smoking. Toss in the sirloin and stir to brown on all sides. Add the onion and cook for 1 minute. Add the potatoes, garlic, thyme, zucchini, tomatoes, and mushrooms; cook over high heat, stirring constantly, until the meat is medium rare, about 5 minutes. Remove to a serving dish. Add the Zinfandel to the juices in the skillet and cook to reduce by half. Swirl in the remaining 2 tablespoons butter, pour sauce over the dish, and serve immediately.

SERVES 4

:: *Pesto and Chèvre–Stuffed Chicken* ::

COUNTRY PESTO
1 bunch fresh basil
3 garlic cloves
4 tablespoons olive oil, or to taste
½ cup pine nuts or walnuts
½ cup grated Parmesan cheese,
   or to taste

4 chicken legs, thighs, and/or breasts
2 ounces Montrachet or similar
   mild chèvre (goat cheese) at room
   temperature
¼ cup pesto, or to taste

To make the pesto: Wash and dry the basil. Strip the leaves from their stems and put in a food processor. Add the garlic and process until leaves are coarsely chopped. Add the remaining ingredients and process until basil is finely chopped and mixture is well blended. Makes about 1 cup. To store, pour a film of olive oil over the pesto surface, cover, and refrigerate for up to 1 week.

To make the chicken: Preheat the oven to 400°F. Mix the chèvre and pesto together until well blended. Slide your fingers between the flesh and skin of the chicken to loosen the skin and stuff the cheese mixture under the skin. Because the skin will shrink during cooking, you may wish to secure the edge of the skin with a small skewer. Salt and pepper the chicken, place in a shallow roasting pan, and roast, uncovered, for about 40 minutes, or until the juices run clear when the chicken is pierced with a skewer.

SERVES 4

Jean-Baptiste Oudry, *The Pàté*, 1743

:: *Sicilian Lemon Chicken* ::

1 chicken, cut into 8 serving pieces.
½ cup olive oil
½ cup fresh lemon juice
¾ cup chopped fresh parsley
3 garlic cloves
½ teaspoon salt
¼ teaspoon freshly ground pepper

This is a traditional family recipe.

Preheat the broiler. Wash and trim the fat from the chicken pieces; lay the pieces in a small roasting pan. In a blender, puree all the remaining ingredients together until smooth. Pour over the chicken, turning to coat evenly. Place the pan about 6 inches from the heating element of the broiler and broil for about 20 minutes, turning the chicken every 5 minutes.

SERVES 4

:: *Vietnamese Lemon Chicken* ::

3 stalks lemongrass, or 1 teaspoon grated
   lemon zest
5 garlic cloves, minced
4 tablespoons Vietnamese fish sauce
3½ tablespoons packed brown sugar
½ teaspoon ground pepper
2 pounds chicken, boned, skinned, and
   cut into 1-inch cubes
2 tablespoons hot water
1 teaspoon fresh lemon juice
1 tablespoon peanut oil
Red pepper flakes to taste

Serve this flavorful stir-fry with steamed rice.

If using the lemongrass, soak it in hot water for 2 hours. Combine the lemongrass or zest with half the garlic, 3 tablespoons of the fish sauce, ½ tablespoon of the sugar, and the pepper and pour over the chicken. Marinate at room temperature for up to 1 hour.

Combine the remaining 3 tablespoons sugar with the hot water in a small saucepan. Cook over medium heat for 3 minutes, or until the mixture starts to caramelize. Stir constantly until amber and steaming. Remove from heat and immediately add the lemon juice.

In a wok or large skillet over high heat, heat the oil, add the garlic, and stir-fry for 10 seconds. Add the chicken and marinade and stir-fry for 3 to 5 minutes. Reduce the heat to medium. Add the remaining 1 tablespoon fish sauce, 2 teaspoons of the caramel mixture, and the red pepper flakes. Stir-fry for 5 minutes. Serve at once.

SERVES 4

:: *Sesame-Ginger Chicken* ::

1 cup light soy sauce

¼ cup water

½ cup dry white wine

1¼ cup packed dark brown sugar

4 garlic cloves, pressed

¼ cup grated fresh ginger

3 tablespoons Asian (toasted) sesame oil

⅓ cup sesame seeds

6 large chicken breast halves, trimmed
 of excess fat

This recipe is a variation on one from a Hawaiian luau cook-book published in the early 1970s. Serve it with rice.

In a medium bowl, combine the soy sauce, water, wine, brown sugar, garlic, and ginger and stir until the brown sugar is dissolved. Using a small whisk, whisk in 2 table-spoons of the sesame oil until emulsified. Oil the bottom and sides of a 9 × 14-inch non-aluminum baking pan with the remaining 1 tablespoon sesame oil. Sprinkle the sesame seeds evenly over the bottom of the pan and place the chicken breasts, skin-side down, on the sesame seeds. Pour the marinade over the chicken, cover, and refriger-ate for at least 1 hour or up to 3 hours.

Remove the chicken from the refrigerator 30 min-utes before cooking. Preheat the broiler. Place the baking pan about 8 inches from the heating element of the broiler and broil the chicken for 15 minutes. Turn the chicken with tongs and broil for another 15 minutes.

SERVES 4 TO 6

:: *Indonesian Chicken Saté* ::

2 tablespoons peanut oil

1 tablespoon curry powder

¼ cup soy sauce

¼ cup chunky peanut butter

1 tablespoon packed light brown sugar

2 tablespoons fresh lime juice

¼ to ½ teaspoon red pepper flakes

1 garlic clove, crushed

1 pound chicken, boned, skinned, and
cut into ¾-inch cubes

PEANUT SAUCE

¼ cup chunky peanut butter

½ cup hot water

¼ to ½ teaspoon red pepper flakes

2 teaspoons molasses

1 tablespoon soy sauce

1 garlic clove, crushed

Few drops of lemon juice

Skewers of tomatoes and green peppers, grilled or broiled with the chicken, make a nice accompaniment. Saté may also be made with cubes of beef or pork.

In a small saucepan, stir the peanut oil and curry powder together. Simmer over low heat for 2 minutes. In a glass baking dish, stir the soy sauce and peanut butter together. Add the curry mixture, brown sugar, lime juice, pepper flakes, and garlic. Add the chicken. Mix well to coat all slices. Cover and refrigerate for at least 4 hours or overnight, turning occasionally.

Remove the chicken from the refrigerator 30 minutes before cooking. Soak 4 bamboo skewers in water for 30 minutes. Light a fire in a charcoal grill, or preheat a gas grill or a broiler. Thread 6 to 7 marinated cubes onto each bamboo skewer. Grill the skewers over a hot fire, turning often, about 20 minutes, or broil about 6 inches from the heating element of the broiler for about 5 to 8 minutes on each side.

To make the peanut sauce: In a small saucepan, mix the peanut butter and water together. Stir in all other ingredients. Simmer for 5 minutes, or until thickened. More water may be added. Serve the saté with the warm sauce alongside.

SERVES 4

Aquamanile (Ewer), Germany,
ca. 1400

:: *Chicken Tikka* ::

3 pounds chicken legs and/or breasts,
  boned, skinned, and cut into 1-inch
  cubes

MARINADE
1 cup plain yogurt
1 teaspoon minced garlic
1 teaspoon ground ginger
2 tablespoons fresh lemon juice
2 tablespoons chili powder
2 tablespoons olive oil
1 teaspoon ground pepper
1 teaspoon salt
Olive oil for brushing

*This Indian dish is good for picnics. Serve it with sliced
tomatoes, onions, and lemon on a bed of lettuce.*

Prick the chicken pieces well with a fork or a sharp knife.
In a large bowl, combine all the marinade ingredients
and blend until smooth. Add the chicken, turn to coat,
cover, and refrigerate for 2 hours.

Remove the chicken from the refrigerator 30 minutes before cooking. Soak 6 wooden skewers in water for
30 minutes. Light a fire in a charcoal grill or preheat a
gas grill. Thread the chicken on the skewers. Brush the
chicken with olive oil and grill on all sides for 6 to 10
minutes.

SERVES 6

:: *Baked Soy Chicken* ::

1 to 1½ pounds skinless, boneless
  chicken, cut into 16 bite-sized chunks
16 very thin lemon slices, seeded
4 white mushrooms cut into 16 slices
12 thin carrot slices
4 tablespoons soy sauce
4 tablespoons mirin or dry sherry

*Be sure that the lemon slices are very thin so they don't over-
power the chicken.*

Preheat the oven to 350°F. Cut four 15-inch-square pieces
of heavy-duty foil. In the center of each square, alter-
nately place alongside each other a piece of chicken, a
slice of lemon, and a slice of mushroom; repeat to use all
the chicken, lemon, and mushrooms. Finally, put 3 carrot
slices on top of the pieces in each square. Spoon 1 tablespoon *each* of soy sauce and mirin or sherry over each
bundle. Fold the sides of the foil over and seal to create
a leakproof packet.

Put the packets in a baking pan and bake for 35
minutes. Open the packets and transfer contents to
individual dishes.

MAKES 4 SERVINGS

Relief from the Tomb of Mentuemhet,
Thebes, ca. 660 B.C.

:: *Chicken and Green Rice Sonoma* ::

1 cup chicken broth

1½ cups long-grain rice

1 cup sparkling wine, preferably a
Sonoma County brand such as Gloria
Ferrer, Korbel, or Piper Sonoma

4 boneless, skinless chicken breast halves

1 tablespoon butter

½ pound mushrooms, sliced

10 ounces frozen chopped spinach,
thawed

Salt and freshly ground pepper to taste

Juice of ½ lemon

1 cup minced fresh parsley, plus 4 sprigs
for garnish

1 tablespoon pesto

In a large saucepan, bring the broth to a boil. Stir in the rice, reduce heat, cover, and simmer for 20 minutes. Meanwhile, bring the wine to a simmer in a nonreactive skillet. Add the chicken, cover, and cook for 10 minutes, turning after 5 minutes. Remove chicken from the wine and set it aside; discard any remaining wine.

Preheat the oven to 350°F. In a medium-heavy saucepan, melt the butter over medium heat, add the mushrooms, cover, and cook for 5 minutes. Stir in the spinach, then the cooked rice. Add the salt, pepper, lemon juice, minced parsley, and pesto. Spread in a buttered or oiled ovenproof dish and place the chicken on top. Bake for 30 minutes. Garnish each chicken breast with a sprig of parsley.

SERVES 4

:: VARIATION

To make a wine sauce for this dish, melt 4 teaspoons butter in a small saucepan. Stir in 3 to 4 teaspoons flour. Cook, stirring, for 3 to 4 minutes. Stir in ½ to 1 cup sparkling wine and cook, stirring constantly, until smooth and thickened.

Edwin Deakin, *Flame Tokay Grapes,*
1884

:: *Pilaf with Chicken and Orange Zest* ::

¼ cup olive oil
2 carrots, peeled and grated
1 onion, finely chopped
Grated zest of 2 oranges
¼ cup sliced almonds
¼ cup raisins
2 skinless, boneless chicken breast halves
  cut into thin strips
¼ teaspoon ground turmeric
1 cup rice, preferably jasmine rice
2 cups chicken broth
Salt to taste
Minced fresh mint for garnish

An adaptation of an Armenian pilaf, this is a very forgiving dish as the ingredient amounts (apart from the rice and water) are not critical, and it doesn't mind sitting on the stove top. Serve with a green salad and warm pita bread.

In a heavy, medium saucepan over low heat, heat the oil. Add the carrots and onion. Cover and cook for 5 to 6 minutes. Add the zest, almonds, raisins, and chicken. Increase heat to medium and sauté for 5 minutes. Sprinkle with the turmeric, stir well, and add the rice. Stir until the rice is coated with oil and turmeric. Add the broth and salt, bring to a boil, reduce heat, cover, and simmer for 20 minutes. Turn off heat and let stand for 5 to 10 minutes. Fluff with a fork, garnish with mint, and serve.

SERVES 4

:: *Piquant Turkey-Spinach Loaf* ::

1 teaspoon butter
½ yellow onion, finely chopped
One-half 10-ounce package frozen
  spinach, thawed and drained
1½ pounds lean ground turkey
½ teaspoon dried thyme
⅓ cup minced fresh parsley
½ cup dried bread crumbs
½ teaspoon ground pepper
¼ teaspoon salt
¾ cup plus ⅓ cup chicken broth
½ teaspoon grated lemon zest
1 tablespoon fresh lemon juice
6 thin lemon slices

David Gilhooly, *My Daily Bread*, 1983

This tasty, low-fat recipe is a good solution to the question "What to do with ground turkey?" Serve with a green salad, dinner rolls, and a good Chardonnay.

Preheat the oven to 350°F. In a small skillet, melt the butter over low heat and sauté the onion until golden. In a large bowl, combine the onion, spinach, turkey, thyme, parsley, bread crumbs, pepper, salt, and ¾ cup broth. Add the lemon zest and juice and mix until well blended. In an 8-inch square baking pan, shape the mixture into a loaf 2 inches high. Bake for 45 to 50 minutes, basting halfway through with the remaining ⅓ cup broth. Serve, garnished with lemon slices.

SERVES 6 TO 8

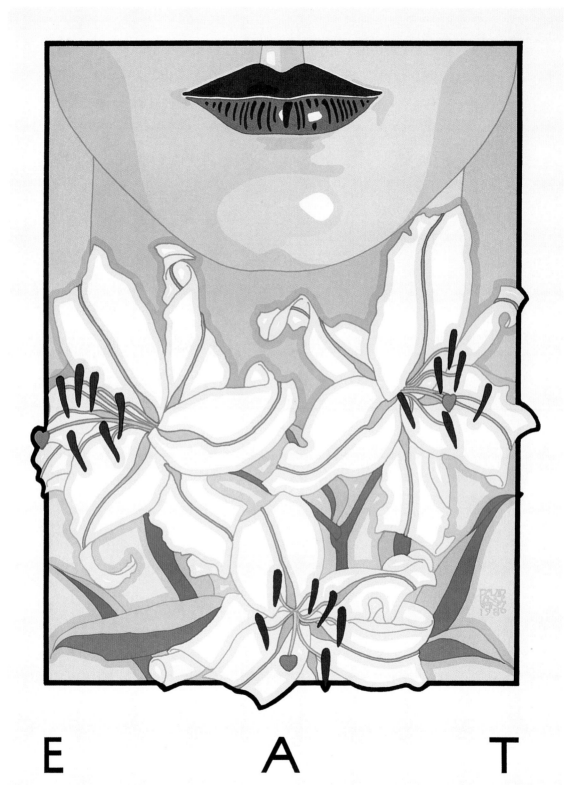

E   A   T

:: *Cioppino* ::

TOMATO BASE

2 tablespoons olive oil

1 onion, chopped

1 green bell pepper, seeded, deribbed, and chopped

Two 28-ounce cans Italian plum tomatoes, drained and chopped (juice reserved)

1 bay leaf

Juice of 2 lemons

2 large fillets orange roughy or sole, cut into 1-inch cubes

1 pound scallops

1 pound medium shrimp, shelled and deveined

1 cracked crab

1 dozen clams, scrubbed

Minced fresh oregano

Salt and freshly ground pepper to taste

Minced fresh parsley for garnish

Your dinner guests will adore this. Serve it with a green salad and sourdough toast.

To make the base: In a large pot over medium heat, heat the olive oil and sauté the onion and pepper until the onion is translucent. Add the tomatoes and their juice, the bay leaf, and lemon juice. Bring to a boil, reduce heat, cover, and simmer for 20 minutes.

Just before serving, add the fish and shellfish. Cover and cook over medium heat until the clams open, about 5 minutes. Discard any clams that do not open. Stir in the oregano and salt and pepper. Serve in large soup bowls, sprinkled with parsley.

SERVES 6

David Lance Goines, *EAT,* 1980

:: *Fish Stew* ::

3 tablespoons olive oil

1 to 2 onions, sliced or chopped

1 to 2 garlic cloves, crushed

2 to 4 red and/or yellow bell peppers, seeded, deribbed, and sliced

2 to 4 celery stalks with leaves, chopped

1 to 3 carrots, peeled and sliced

1 bay leaf

¼ to ½ cup parsley, chopped

2 sprigs fresh thyme

4 to 6 tomatoes, peeled, seeded, and chopped, or 28 ounces canned Italian (plum) tomatoes, drained and chopped (juice reserved)

½ cup dry white wine, or more as needed

½ to 1 cup fish stock or clam broth

½ to 1 pound salmon fillets, boned

1 pound firm white fish, such as halibut or sea bass

¼ pound bay scallops, rinsed

1 pound large or medium shrimp, shelled and deveined

¼ pound fresh lump crabmeat (optional)

2 pounds clams or mussels, scrubbed (debeard mussels)

Good for a buffet, but also very nice served at the table from a tureen or large casserole. Have lots of fresh crusty bread to mop up the juices. Serve with a simple green salad and a Sauvignon Blanc or a white Côtes du Rhône. Leftover stew freezes well and makes a great pasta sauce.

In a large pot over medium heat, heat the olive oil and sauté the onions until limp. Add the garlic, peppers, celery, carrots. Cook for a few minutes. Add the herbs, tomatoes and juice, wine, and stock or broth. Bring to a boil, reduce heat, and simmer for 30 to 40 minutes.

Sear the salmon in an oiled hot skillet, skin-side down, just long enough to make the skin stick to the pan and come off easily. Cut the salmon into pieces. Cut the white fish into pieces, removing any bones. About 10 minutes before serving time, raise the heat slightly and heat the broth. Add the fish, then the scallops, shrimp, crabmeat, and lastly the clams and/or mussels. Cover and cook just until the clams and/or mussels open, about 5 minutes. Discard any clams or mussels that do not open. Serve in wide flat soup dishes, over steamed white rice or simple pasta, or as is.

SERVES 8 TO 10

Arnold Genthe, *A Sidewalk Kitchen,* 1906

:: *Shrimp with Feta Cheese* ::

2 tablespoons butter

2 tablespoons olive oil

2 garlic cloves, crushed

1 tablespoon minced fresh rosemary

1 bunch green onions, thinly sliced,
   including green portions

¾ pound mushrooms, thickly sliced

¼ cup dry white wine

Juice of 1 lemon

1 lemon, thinly sliced

½ cup black olives, drained and pitted

3 Roma plum tomatoes, quartered

½ pound jumbo shrimp, shelled,
   deveined, and butterflied

½ pound feta cheese, crumbled (about
   ½ cup)

This colorful, simple Greek dish based on a Cliff House recipe can be served with a rice pilaf with pine nuts.

In a large skillet, melt the butter with the oil over medium heat. Add the garlic, rosemary, and green onions. Cook, stirring constantly for 2 minutes. Add the mushrooms and cook until softened. Add the wine, lemon juice, half of the lemon slices, the olives, and tomatoes. Heat through over high heat. Add the shrimp and cook, stirring constantly, until the shrimp turn pink. Remove from heat and quickly stir in the feta cheese. Serve at once.

SERVES 2 TO 3

:: *Baked Swordfish with Onion, Mushrooms, and Dill* ::

½ pound mushrooms, sliced

1 onion, sliced

2 tablespoons extra virgin olive oil

2 tablespoons fresh lemon juice

6 tablespoons minced fresh dill, or 2
   tablespoons dried dill

Two 1-inch thick swordfish steaks

4 small bay leaves

4 slices tomato

A delicious way of cooking swordfish.

Preheat the oven to 425°F. In a medium bowl, toss the mushrooms and onion with the olive oil, lemon juice, and dill. Place half of the mushroom mixture in a glass baking dish. Cut each swordfish steak into 2 pieces and place the fish on top of the mushroom mixture in the baking dish. Place 1 bay leaf on each piece of fish and cover with a tomato slice. Pour the remaining mushroom mixture over the fish. Seal the dish with aluminum foil and bake for 30 minutes.

SERVES 4

Red-Figure Hydria (Water Jar),
Athens, ca. 480–450 B.C.

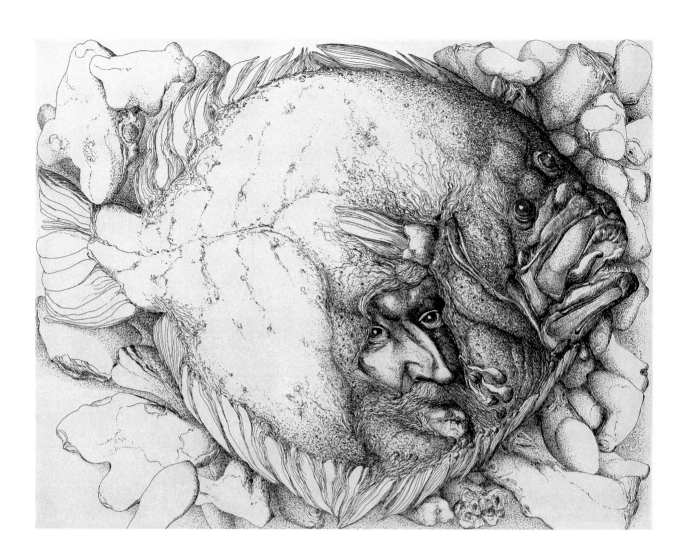

:: *Ed's Salmon* ::

½ cup alderwood chips (optional)
4 salmon fillets, boned
Salt and freshly ground pepper to taste
¼ cup dry white wine
1 or 2 tablespoons fresh lemon juice
4 tablespoons butter
Minced fresh rosemary and oregano
  to taste
Paprika to taste
Minced fresh parsley for garnish

No idea who Ed is, but his salmon is wonderful. The salmon can also be broiled in the oven or even pan-fried using this marinade. Salmon steaks can be used in place of fillets.

Light a fire in a charcoal grill. Soak the alderwood chips in water, if using. Lightly salt and pepper the salmon and set aside in a baking dish. In a small saucepan, combine the wine, lemon juice, and butter. Add the herbs and paprika. Heat to melt the butter and blend the flavors. Pour over fish, turn to coat, and let stand at room temperature for about 15 minutes.

When the coals are lightly covered with gray ash, drain the wood chips and sprinkle them over the coals. Place the fish, skin-side down, on the grill and cook for 2 to 3 minutes. Turn and cook another 5 to 6 minutes, or until opaque on the outside but translucent at the very center. Sprinkle with minced parsley.

SERVES 4

:: *Stuffed Fillet of Sole* ::

¼ pound bay scallops, finely chopped
¼ cup dried bread crumbs
1 teaspoon minced garlic
¼ cup minced fresh parsley
4 tablespoons butter, melted
6 sole fillets
¼ cup dry sherry

Preheat the oven to 375°F. Mix the scallops, bread crumbs, garlic, parsley, and half the butter together; spread on the sole fillets and roll up. Place the fillets in a buttered 9-inch square glass baking dish. Brush the fillets with the remaining butter. Cover with aluminum foil and bake for 20 minutes. Add the sherry, re-cover, and bake for 10 minutes.

SERVES 6

Gunter Grass, *Man in Flounder,* 1978

Breads

:: *Peasant Cheese Bread* ::

1 package (2 teaspoons) active dry yeast

1½ tablespoons sugar

⅓ cup warm (105° to 115°F) water

1 cup warm (105° to 115°F) milk

1 egg

2 teaspoons salt

2 tablespoons whole wheat flour

2 tablespoons buckwheat flour

3¼ to 3½ cups unbleached all-purpose
  or bread flour

½ cup (1 stick) unsalted butter, at room
  temperature, cut into pieces

CHEESE FILLING

4 cups (1 pound) shredded Muenster
  cheese

4 cups (1 pound) shredded Monterey
  jack cheese, plain or flavored

1 egg

2 tablespoons unsalted butter, melted

Cornmeal for sprinkling pan

1 egg beaten with 1 tablespoon milk

2 tablespoons sesame seeds

Peasant cheese bread is a stuffed bread formed by twisting the top edges of the dough to make a folded topknot. This impressive-looking loaf is traditionally sold by vendors and eaten out of hand in Eastern Europe and Georgia. Serve it alongside seasonal greens with walnuts and pears, a cabbage salad with slivers of prosciutto, or a hearty vegetable soup.

In a small bowl, sprinkle the yeast and a pinch of the sugar over the warm water. Stir to dissolve and let stand until foamy, about 10 minutes. In a large bowl or the work bowl of a heavy-duty electric mixer fitted with the paddle attachment, combine the milk, egg, remaining sugar, salt, whole wheat flour, buckwheat flour, and 1½ cups of the unbleached flour. Beat by hand with a whisk or with the mixer until creamy. Add the yeast mixture and beat for 1 minute. Add 1 cup flour and the butter. Beat until smooth. Add the remaining flour ½ cup at a time, changing to a wooden spoon when necessary if mixing by hand, until a shaggy, yet soft, workable dough is formed that just clears the sides of the bowl.

Turn the dough out onto a lightly floured work surface and knead vigorously until elastic, smooth, and satiny, about 3 minutes, adding 1 tablespoon of flour at a time as necessary to prevent sticking. Place in a greased deep container, turn once to coat the top, and cover with plastic wrap. Let stand in a warm place until doubled or tripled in volume, about 1½ hours.

Meanwhile, prepare the filling by combining all the ingredients and mixing until evenly blended. Refrigerate until use. Line the bottom of a 9-inch springform pan with a circle of parchment paper. Grease the paper and sides of the pan and sprinkle the greased surfaces lightly with cornmeal.

PAGE 114 Jasper Johns, *Bread,* 1969

Turn the dough out onto a lightly floured work surface. Pat into a thick circle and roll the dough out into a circle about 24 inches in diameter. If the dough resists rolling, cover it lightly with a towel and let it rest for about 10 minutes.

Fold the dough gently into quarters and transfer it to the prepared pan. Unfold immediately, arrange the dough evenly over the pan, and press it into the bottom, allowing the excess to hang over the edges. Spoon in the filling, mounding it slightly higher in the center. Pick up sections of the overhanging dough and lay it in even pleats over the filling, rotating the pan as you go. Gather the ends together and twist to form a topknot. Pinch together any torn dough. Let stand at room temperature for 20 minutes. Preheat the oven to 375°F.

Twist the topknot to tighten it and brush the dough with the egg and milk mixture. Sprinkle with sesame seeds. Place on the lowest rack of the oven and bake for 50 to 60 minutes, or until golden brown.

Let cool in the pan on a wire rack for 15 minutes before removing the pan sides. Let cool to room temperature before serving. This bread may be wrapped in plastic and stored up to 3 days in the refrigerator.

MAKES ONE 9-INCH ROUND LOAF

:: *Panini alla Polenta* ::

SPONGE

1 package (2 teaspoons) active dry yeast

Pinch of sugar

2 cups warm (105° to 115°F) water

½ cup whole wheat flour

2 cups unbleached bread flour

DOUGH

2 to 2¼ cups unbleached bread flour

¼ cup good olive oil

2 teaspoons salt

¼ cup wheat bran

½ cup polenta

Cornmeal for sprinkling pan

These Italian cornmeal and whole wheat rolls are crusty and savory, and are best eaten the same day they are baked. Eat plain with fruit and Bel Paese cheese or alongside antipasto, roast poultry, pastas, and crisp salads.

To make the sponge: In a large bowl or the work bowl of a heavy-duty electric mixer fitted with the paddle attachment, sprinkle the yeast and sugar over the warm water. Stir to dissolve. Add the whole wheat and bread flours. Beat with a whisk or the mixer until smooth. Cover loosely with plastic wrap and let stand at a room temperature for 2 to 4 hours. The sponge will be bubbly. It can be stored for 1 day in the refrigerator before using, if necessary.

To make the dough: Add 1 cup of the unbleached flour, the olive oil, salt, bran, and polenta to the sponge and beat hard by hand with a whisk, or on medium speed in an electric mixer until elastic, about 1 minute. Continue to beat in the remaining flour, ¼ cup at a time, to form a soft dough that just pulls away from the sides of the bowl, switching to a wooden spoon when necessary if making by hand.

Turn the dough out onto a lightly floured work surface and knead vigorously until elastic yet still moist and slightly tacky, about 3 to 4 minutes, adding 1 tablespoon of flour at a time as necessary to prevent sticking.

Put the dough in an oiled deep container, turn once to coat the top, and cover with plastic wrap. Let rise in a warm place until doubled or tripled in volume, about 2 hours.

Turn the dough out onto the work surface. Divide the dough into 16 equal pieces. Shape each piece into a tight round. Place about 1 inch apart on greased or parchment-lined baking sheets sprinkled with cornmeal and a bit of whole-wheat flour. Dust the tops with a bit of unbleached flour for a rustic look. Cover loosely with a layer of plastic wrap and let stand at room temperature until doubled, about 45 minutes.

Twenty minutes before baking, preheat the oven to 425°F, with or without a baking stone. With floured kitchen shears, snip the top of each roll 2 or 3 times. Bake for 10 minutes. Reduce the oven heat to 350°F and bake for 8 to 12 minutes, or until browned and hollow sounding when tapped. Serve immediately.

MAKES 16 ROLLS

:: *Ricotta Bread* ::

2 cups (16 ounces) ricotta cheese
1 egg, beaten
1 cup (4 ounces) grated Parmesan cheese
½ teaspoon salt
⅛ teaspoon ground pepper
2 teaspoons minced fresh parsley
1 loaf French bread, cut into ½-inch slices

Preheat the oven to 375°F. In a medium bowl, mix all the ingredients except the bread together until well blended. Spread the ricotta mixture on the bread slices and place them on a baking sheet. Bake for 15 minutes, or until lightly browned.

MAKES ABOUT 30 SLICES

:: Laurie's Puffed Pancake ::

½ cup milk
½ cup all-purpose flour
2 eggs
Pinch of ground nutmeg
4 tablespoons butter
Confectioners' sugar
Juice of ½ lemon

This recipe comes from Robin Williams's mother, Laurie Williams. It makes a giant puffed pancake that is great for breakfast or brunch. Serve with maple syrup, jelly, jam, or marmalade.

Preheat the oven to 425°F. In a medium bowl, beat the milk, flour, eggs, and nutmeg together until just mixed. In a 12-inch ovenproof skillet, melt the butter over medium heat. When the butter bubbles begin to subside, pour in the batter. Bake the pancake for 15 to 20 minutes, or until brown and puffed. Dust with confectioners' sugar and return to the oven for 1 minute. Remove from the oven and sprinkle with lemon juice. Serve at once.

SERVES 4 TO 6

:: The Food Lady's Muffins ::

½ to ¾ cup whole wheat flour
2½ cups sifted unbleached all-purpose flour
2¼ teaspoons baking soda
2¼ teaspoons ground cinnamon
¾ cup canola oil
3 eggs
½ cup buttermilk
2 teaspoons vanilla extract
1¼ pounds carrots, peeled and coarsely shredded
½ cup raisins and/or walnuts

Healthy carrot muffins, good for a hungry crowd.

Preheat the oven to 350°F. Line 24 muffin cups with paper. In a medium bowl, mix the flours, baking soda, and cinnamon together. In another medium bowl, beat the oil, eggs, buttermilk, and vanilla together. Stir the wet ingredients into the dry ingredients until just blended; the batter should be lumpy. Stir in the carrots, raisins, and/or walnuts just to blend. Fill the lined muffin cups three-fourths full. Bake for about 40 minutes, or until lightly browned.

MAKES 22 TO 24 MUFFINS

Worcester Plates, 1780–85

Breads

:: *Orange-Raisin Scones* ::

1 cup raisins

1 cup orange juice

½ cup sugar, plus more for sprinkling

3 cups unbleached all-purpose flour

4 teaspoons baking powder

1 teaspoon cream of tartar

½ cup shortening

1 egg

These are great for breakfast or with tea. Serve warm with preserves or honey.

Preheat the oven to 400°F. Grease 2 baking sheets. Soak the raisins in the orange juice.

In a large bowl, stir the ½ cup sugar, the flour, baking powder, and cream of tartar together. Using a pastry cutter or 2 knives, cut the shortening into the flour mixture until it forms crumbs the size of peas. Add the raisins, juice, and egg and stir until blended. Shape the dough into a ball.

On a lightly floured surface, pat the dough into a 10 × 14-inch rectangle. Cut in half lengthwise, then cut the 2 pieces crosswise to make 12 squares. Cut the squares in half diagonally to make 24 triangles. Place the triangles 1 inch apart on the prepared pans. Sprinkle with sugar and bake for 12 minutes, or until golden brown

MAKES 2 DOZEN

:: *Café Scones* ::

2 cups unbleached all-purpose flour

¼ cup granulated sugar

1 teaspoon baking soda

2 teaspoons cream of tartar

½ teaspoon salt

2 ounces unsalted butter

2 ounces margarine

1 large egg

1 egg yolk

3 tablespoons milk

½ cup currants

3 ounces half-and-half

¼ cup brown sugar

Nicolas Lancret, *Breakfast before the Hunt*, ca. 1740

Sift the flour, sugar, baking soda, cream of tartar, and salt together into a large bowl. Cut in the butter and margarine with a pastry cutter or 2 knives until the mixture is the texture of coarse meal. In a medium bowl beat the egg, egg yolk, and milk together until well blended. Add to the dry ingredients and stir until just blended; do not overmix! Add the currants and stir until just evenly distributed. On a lightly floured board, roll out into a ¾-inch circle. Wrap the dough in wax paper and refrigerate for 30 minutes.

Preheat the oven to 350°F. Remove the dough from the refrigerator and brush with the half-and-half. Sprinkle the brown sugar on top and cut into 8 wedges. Line a baking sheet with parchment paper. Place the dough on the prepared pan and bake for 14 to 18 minutes. Transfer to wire racks. Serve warm or at room temperature.

SERVES 8

Breads

:: *Wieniec* ::

1 cup milk

3 packages (2 tablespoons) active
 dry yeast

10 tablespoons sugar

½ cup (1 stick) butter at room
 temperature

3 eggs

1 egg yolk

5 to 6 cups unbleached all-purpose flour

Pinch of salt

2 egg whites, slightly beaten

FROSTING

1 tablespoon butter at room temperature

1 cup confectioners' sugar

1 teaspoon vanilla extract

1 to 2 teaspoons milk

Pronounced veen yetz, *this is a holiday or Christmas sweet bread from Poland.*

Heat the milk to lukewarm (105° to 115°F). Mix in the yeast and 3 tablespoons of the sugar. Let stand for 5 minutes. In a large bowl, cream the butter and the remaining 7 tablespoons sugar together until fluffy. Beat the eggs and egg yolk together. Add to the creamed mixture and mix well. Stir in the yeast mixture. Stir in the flour ½ cup at a time until the dough pulls away from the side of the bowl. On a lightly floured board, knead for about 10 minutes until the dough is smooth and elastic, adding more flour 1 tablespoon at a time as needed to keep the dough from sticking. Place in a greased bowl, and turn to coat the top, cover with a damp cloth or plastic wrap, and let rise in a warm place for about 2 hours, or until doubled in bulk.

On a floured board, cut the dough into 3 even pieces. Form the dough into 3 strips about 12 inches long. Braid and shape into horseshoe. Pinch the ends to close. Place on a greased baking sheet. Brush with the egg whites and let rise again, about 25 minutes.

Preheat the oven to 400°F. Bake until golden brown, about 30 minutes. Let cool on a wire rack.

Mix all the frosting ingredients together until the mixture is of spreading consistency. Spread over the top of the bread, letting it drip down the sides. Let the frosting set before slicing.

MAKES 1 LOAF

Goblet, London, 1590

:: *Sour Cream Coffee Cake with Apricot Filling* ::

1 cup sugar

½ cup (1 stick) butter at room
  temperature

2 eggs

1 cup (8 ounces) sour cream

1 teaspoon vanilla extract

2 cups unbleached all-purpose flour

1 teaspoon baking soda

1 teaspoon baking powder

¼ teaspoon salt

1 cup apricot pastry filling, preferably
  Solo brand (available at many supermarkets), or any pie filling

TOPPING

½ cup chopped walnuts or pecans

¼ cup sugar

1 teaspoon ground cinnamon

Preheat the oven to 350°F. Grease and flour a 10-inch tube pan.

In a medium bowl, cream the sugar and butter together until fluffy. Add the eggs, sour cream, and vanilla and beat to blend well. Sift the flour, baking soda, baking powder, and salt together. Gradually stir the dry ingredients into the butter mixture; do not overbeat. Pour half the batter into the prepared pan. Pour the apricot filling on top of the batter. Top with the remaining batter.

Mix all the topping ingredients together and sprinkle over the cake batter. Push the nuts into the batter slightly. Bake for 45 minutes, or until lightly browned or a tester inserted in the center comes out clean. Let cool for 5 to 10 minutes in the pan. Turn the cake out onto a rack and cool completely.

MAKES 10 TO 16 SLICES

Fichu of Point de France Lace (detail),
France, 1700–20

:: *Lemon Bread* ::

6 tablespoons butter at room
  temperature
1 cup sugar
2 eggs
½ cup milk
Grated zest of 2 lemons
1½ cups unbleached all-purpose flour
1 teaspoon baking powder
¼ teaspoon salt
½ cup chopped pecans

TOPPING
1 cup sugar
Juice of 1 to 1½ lemons

Preheat the oven to 350°F. Grease and flour a 9 × 5-inch loaf pan.

In a large bowl, cream the butter and sugar together until fluffy. Beat in the eggs, milk, and zest. In a medium bowl, stir the flour, baking powder, and salt together. Gradually stir into the butter mixture. Stir in the pecans just until blended. Pour into the prepared pan. Bake for 50 minutes, or until a cake tester inserted in the center comes out clean.

Combine the topping ingredients and pour over the hot bread. Let cool in the pan for 1 hour.

MAKES 1 LOAF

Wayne Thiebaud, *Lunch,* 1967

Sauces and Condiments

:: *Mustard Sauce* ::

1¼ cups packed brown sugar
1 cup apple cider vinegar
1 cup dry mustard
2 eggs
1 teaspoon ground cloves
½ teaspoon ground turmeric
¼ teaspoon salt (optional)

Delicious with grilled chicken or sausage.

In a medium saucepan, mix all the ingredients together thoroughly until smooth. Heat over low heat, stirring constantly, until thickened, 5 to 8 minutes. Pour into a hot, sterilized pint jar. Let cool and store in the refrigerator for up to 2 months.

MAKES 1 PINT

:: *Chili Sauce* ::

3 pounds tomatoes
1½ onions, finely chopped
1½ large green bell peppers, seeded, deribbed, and finely chopped
1 jalapeño chili, seeded (optional)
1 cup apple cider vinegar
¾ cup sugar
2 teaspoons salt
¾ teaspoon *each* ground cloves, cinnamon, and allspice

Good on hamburgers, scrambled eggs, and meat loaf.

Blanch the tomatoes in a large pot of boiling water for 1 minute. Using a slotted spoon, transfer to a bowl of cold water. Drain, core, and peel the tomatoes. Cut each in half crosswise and squeeze upside down to shake out the seeds. Chop the tomatoes.

In a large saucepan, combine all the ingredients. Bring to a boil, reduce heat, and simmer, uncovered, for 2½ hours, or until thickened. Pour the hot mixture into 3 hot, sterilized pint jars and seal. Store in the refrigerator.

MAKES ABOUT 3 PINTS

PAGE 130 Peter Carl Fabergé,
Tea Service and Table, 1896–1908

Paul Storr, *Silver Sauceboat,* 1819

:: *Modega* ::

2 cups fine fresh French bread crumbs

1 cup (4 ounces) grated Parmesan cheese

1 cup minced fresh parsley

Olive oil to moisten crumbs, cheese, and
parsley

Salt and freshly ground pepper

6 garlic cloves, minced

*Use this herbed crumb and cheese mixture to bread chicken
or fish before baking, or for stuffing artichokes or tomatoes.*

Mix all of the ingredients together in a large bowl.
Store in an airtight container in the refrigerator for
up to 1 month.

MAKES ABOUT 4 CUPS

:: *Spiced Kumquats* ::

2 cups kumquats
Whole cloves
2 cups sugar
2 cups water
1 cinnamon stick

The kumquats will keep for many months, and their flavor improves with age. Serve them as a garnish for duck, chicken, pork, and ham, or sliced in salads and fruit compotes. When the kumquats are used up, the syrup makes a delicious poaching liquid for pears.

Cover the kumquats with boiling water and steep for 2 minutes. Drain and let cool briefly. Stick a whole clove into the stem end of each kumquat. Combine the sugar and water in a large saucepan and bring to a boil. Add the kumquats and the cinnamon stick to the sugar syrup. Lower the heat and poach gently for 20 minutes. Let cool. Pour into a hot, sterilized quart glass jar and store in the refrigerator.

MAKES 1 QUART

:: *Pear Chutney* ::

2 pounds Anjou or Bartlett pears,
  peeled, cored, and cut into
  ⅛-inch-thick slices
¼ cup cider vinegar
¼ cup sugar
¼ pound golden raisins
¼ cup finely chopped onions
1 tablespoon minced fresh ginger
1 tablespoon mustard seeds
1 teaspoon salt
½ tablespoon minced garlic
¾ teaspoon red pepper flakes

J. Paul Verrees, *The Kaiser Is Canned—Can Food*, 1918

Serve with grilled chicken or duck, savory sausages, or roast or smoked turkey sandwiches.

Combine all the ingredients in an airtight non-aluminum container and refrigerate overnight. The next day, preheat the oven to 375°F. Pour all the ingredients into a large Dutch oven or heavy, flameproof casserole. Place over medium-high heat, uncovered, and bring to a boil. Place in the oven and bake, uncovered, for 40 minutes, or until no juices remain. Remove from the oven, divide among 4 hot, sterilized half-pint jars, and seal. Store in the refrigerator for up to 1 month.

MAKES 2 PINTS

:: *Kiwi Chutney* ::

8 ripe kiwi fruits, peeled and sliced
1½ onions, thinly sliced
½ lemon, seeded and thinly sliced
1 ounce candied ginger (crystallized),
  thinly sliced
¾ teaspoon ground ginger
½ cup raisins
¾ teaspoon salt
¼ teaspoon cayenne pepper, or to taste
1 pound light brown sugar
⅓ cup distilled white vinegar

Good with meats or mixed with cream cheese as a spread for appetizers or sandwiches.

Combine all the ingredients in a heavy, medium non-aluminum pot; simmer for 2 hours, stirring often, especially after the chutney cooks down. (The mixture will turn dark brown and smell heavenly after 1 hour.) Divide among 4 hot, sterilized half-pint jars and refrigerate for up to 1 month.

MAKES 2 PINTS

:: *Sonoma Chutney* ::

2 cups chopped apples
2 cups chopped green tomatoes
1 cup chopped white onion
1 cup raisins
1 cup packed brown sugar
¾ teaspoon ground ginger, or
  1 tablespoon grated fresh ginger
¾ teaspoon ground allspice
½ teaspoon ground pepper
1 garlic clove, crushed
1 cup white wine vinegar

Combine the apples, tomatoes, onion, raisins, brown sugar, spices, garlic and ½ cup of the vinegar in a large heavy non-aluminum pot. Bring to a boil, reduce heat, and simmer for 1 hour, stirring frequently and gradually adding the remaining ½ cup vinegar. Pour into 4 hot, sterilized half-pint glass jars, seal, and store in the refrigerator for up to 1 month.

MAKES 2 PINTS

:: *Orange-Lime Marmalade* ::

5 whole oranges, sliced (4 cups)
2 small lemons
1 or 2 Rangpur limes
3 cups water
6 cups sugar
½ cup fresh lemon juice

This tart marmalade is both beautiful and delicious. Try it on your breakfast toast.

Thinly slice the oranges, lemons, and limes, discarding the seeds. Cover the fruit with the water; let stand overnight. In a large non-aluminum pot, bring to a boil and cook, uncovered, for 40 minutes, stirring occasionally. Let stand for 4 hours. Add the sugar and bring to a boil, stirring constantly. Boil, stirring occasionally, for 20 minutes or until the mixture sheets off a spoon or registers 220°F on a candy thermometer. Add the lemon juice. Pour into 7 hot, sterilized half-pint jars and seal. Store in the refrigerator.

MAKES 7 HALF-PINTS

:: *Fig Jam* ::

2 quarts (4 to 5 pounds) fresh figs, stemmed and chopped
1 lemon (or orange), coarsely chopped
1 cinnamon stick
4 cups sugar

This recipe is from a nineteenth-century California farming family.

Preheat the oven to 325°F. Combine the figs, lemon or orange, and cinnamon stick in a Dutch oven or heavy casserole. Bake for 1½ to 2 hours, stirring every 30 minutes. Stir in the sugar. Bake another 1½ to 2 hours, stirring every 30 minutes. The jam is done when a sample chilled in the freezer for 15 minutes shows popped bubbles that do not refill. Pour into 4 hot, sterilized jars, seal, and refrigerate.

MAKES 4 PINTS

Desserts

:: *Stuffed Poached Pears with Caramel Sauce* ::

8 firm pears (Anjou or Bosc)
4 cups fruity white wine
2 cups water
2 lemons, halved

CARAMEL SAUCE
¼ cup sugar
2 cups heavy cream
Pinch of salt

¾ cup walnuts, toasted
2 ounces Gorgonzola

Pears stuffed with Gorgonzola and walnuts make an elegant dessert for a dinner party in winter, when Anjou pears are at their best. It can be prepared the day before; warm the sauce just before serving.

Peel the pears, leaving the stems intact, and cut a slice from the bottom of each pear to allow it to stand upright. Using a teaspoon or a small melon baller, core the pears from the bottom. Combine the wine, water, and lemons in a large non-aluminum pot. Bring to a boil. Add the pears, reduce heat and simmer until the pears are just tender when pierced with the tip of a knife. Let cool in the liquid.

To make the sauce: In a medium, heavy pan melt the sugar over medium heat and cook until amber in color. Add the cream and salt. Bring to a boil and cook to reduce until the mixture just coats the back of a spoon; watch carefully and reduce heat, if necessary, to keep it from boiling over. Remove from heat and keep warm over barely simmering water.

To serve, remove the pears from the liquid and pat dry with paper towels. Stuff each pear with alternating spoonfuls of walnuts and Gorgonzola, finishing with Gorgonzola to seal. Stand each pear upright in the center of a small plate. Coat each pear completely with the sauce, letting it flow onto plate. Serve at once.

SERVES 8

PAGE 138 Raphaelle Peale,
Blackberries (detail), ca. 1813

:: Gingered Peaches ::

1 pound ripe fresh peaches
4 or 5 pieces candied (crystallized)
  ginger, finely diced
Crème fraîche for serving

Try serving this with crème anglaise (custard sauce) instead of the crème fraîche.

Blanch the peaches in boiling water for 1 to 2 minutes. Transfer to a bowl of cold water. Drain. Peel, pit, and slice peaches into a serving bowl. Add the ginger. Cover and let sit at room temperature for at least 1 hour. Serve with a dollop of crème fraîche.

SERVES 4 TO 6

:: Fruit and Berry Cooler ::

BERRY WINE SAUCE
10 ounces unsweetened frozen raspberries
1½ cups unsweetened cranberry juice
¾ cup sugar
3 tablespoons cornstarch
½ cup dry red wine

4 pints mixed sherbets such as lemon,
  raspberry, orange, lime
About 4 cups fresh fruits such as
  blueberries, strawberries, raspberries,
  grapes

The sauce is delicious and keeps for several weeks in the refrigerator.

In a medium saucepan, combine the raspberries and cranberry juice and bring to a boil. Using the back of a large spoon press the mixture through a sieve to remove all the seeds and pulp. Return the puree to the saucepan. Mix the sugar and cornstarch together in a small bowl. Add to the puree. Cook and stir over medium-low heat until thickened and bubbly. Remove from heat and stir in the wine. Let cool, then cover and refrigerate for at least 1 hour.

Serve 3 small scoops of sherbet in each serving dish. Arrange a few spoonfuls of fresh fruit over the top of the sherbet in each serving and ladle some sauce over the fruit. Serve at once.

SERVES 10

:: *Cold Lemon Soufflé* ::

1 envelope (1 tablespoon) plain gelatin
¼ cup cold water
3 egg yolks
1 cup sugar
Grated zest of 2 large lemons
¼ cup fresh lemon juice
4 egg whites
1¾ cups heavy cream

Serve in a shallow pool of raspberry sauce, if you like.

In a cup, mix the gelatin with the water. In a large bowl, beat the egg yolks with the sugar until pale and thick. Beat in the lemon zest and juice. Set aside. In a large bowl, beat the egg whites until stiff, glossy peaks form. In a deep bowl, beat the cream until stiff peaks form,

Dissolve the gelatin mixture in a double boiler over simmering water; fold into the lemon mixture. Fold the beaten egg whites, then the whipped cream into the yolk mixture until well blended. Pour into a 6-cup serving dish or soufflé dish. Refrigerate until firm and cold, at least 4 hours or preferably overnight.

SERVES 8

:: *The Lemon Thing* ::

2 cups heavy cream
½ cup fresh lemon juice
½ cup sweetened condensed milk
½ cup sugar
Pinch of salt
Lemon zest curls, made with a zester,
   for garnish

This delicious dessert is not for the calorie-conscious, but it is lovely at the end of a light summer lunch.

In a large, deep bowl, beat the cream, lemon juice, and milk until soft peaks form. Refrigerate for 2 hours. Stir in the sugar and beat until very thick. Add the salt. Cover and refrigerate for at least 2 hours. Decorate with lemon zest.

SERVES 4 GENEROUSLY

Anne Vallayer-Coster, *Still Life with Plums and a Lemon*, 1778

Desserts

:: *Frozen Grand Marnier Mousse* ::

9 almond macaroons
¼ cup Grand Marnier or Triple
　Sec liqueur
1½ quarts vanilla ice cream, softened
1 cup fresh raspberries, sliced fresh
　strawberries, or raspberry sauce
½ cup (2 ounces) slivered almonds,
　toasted

Quick and simple to make, but delicious.

Crumble the macaroons and soak them in the liqueur. Mix into the softened ice cream. Pour into an 8-cup soufflé dish, or 8 metal cupcake liners or individual serving dishes, and freeze. Serve topped with berries or raspberry sauce and toasted almonds.

SERVES 8

:: *Cranberry Ice* ::

4 cups (1 pound) cranberries
2 cups water
2 cups sugar
Juice of 2 lemons, strained

This is a fine accompaniment to a holiday turkey dinner. It is refreshing with fruit salad and good as a dessert with cookies.

Rinse and pick over the berries. In a large saucepan, combine the berries and water. Bring to a boil and cook until the berries pop, about 10 minutes. Push through a fine-meshed sieve into a bowl, using the back of a large spoon. Return to the pan and add the sugar. Bring to a boil and cook, stirring, until the sugar is thoroughly dissolved. Let cool. Stir in the lemon juice. Pour into a container and freeze. It's not necessary to stir this while freezing.

SERVES 6

Bertha Lum, *Green Dragon Cocktail,*
1937

:: Chocolate Fudge Pudding Cake ::

1 cup sifted all-purpose flour

2 teaspoons baking powder

½ teaspoon salt

¾ cup sugar

3 tablespoons plus ¼ cup unsweetened
  cocoa powder

1 teaspoon vanilla extract

½ cup milk

2 tablespoons vegetable oil

½ cup (or more) coarsely chopped
  pecans

1¼ cups packed brown sugar

2 cups hot water

Whipped cream and chocolate sprinkles
  for garnish (optional)

Preheat the oven to 350°F. Sift the flour, baking powder, salt, sugar, and 3 tablespoons cocoa together into a medium bowl. In a small bowl, combine the vanilla, milk, and oil. Stir into the dry ingredients until well blended. Stir in the nuts. Pour into an 8-inch square pan.

In a small bowl, combine the brown sugar with the remaining ¼ cup cocoa. Mix to blend and sprinkle over the batter. Gently pour the hot water over the top. Bake for 40 to 45 minutes, or until set.

Spoon into individual bowls and top with whipped cream and chocolate sprinkles, if you like.

SERVES 4 TO 6

:: Minetry's Miracle ::

2 cups (4 sticks) butter

2 cups sugar

12 eggs, separated

10 ounces amaretti (about 48 cookies)

1 cup bourbon

4 ounces (4 squares) unsweetened
  chocolate, melted

1 teaspoon vanilla extract

1 cup chopped pecans

24 double ladyfingers, split lengthwise

1½ cups heavy cream, whipped

Vessel for Drinking Chocolate, Maya,
Guatemala, A.D. 600

This obscenely rich dessert is divine.

In a large bowl, cream the butter and sugar together until light and fluffy. Beat the egg yolks until light and beat into the creamed mixture. Soak the amaretti in the bourbon. Beat the chocolate into the butter mixture. Add the vanilla and pecans. In a large bowl, beat the egg whites until stiff, glossy peaks form. Fold into chocolate mixture.

Line the sides and bottom of a 10- or 12-inch spring-form pan with the ladyfingers, split side up. Alternate layers of soaked amaretti and chocolate mixture in the lined pan. Cover and refrigerate for at least 8 hours, or overnight. Remove the sides of the pan. Decorate the top with the whipped cream.

SERVES 16 TO 20

:: *Cornmeal Crepes with Berries* ::

3 cups sliced fresh strawberries
2 tablespoons granulated sugar
1 teaspoon Grand Marnier liqueur
  (optional)
1 cup milk
3 large eggs
¼ cup yellow cornmeal
⅔ cup all-purpose flour
1 teaspoon vanilla extract
½ teaspoon salt
4 to 5 tablespoons butter
⅓ cup apricot jam
2 cups sour cream
Melted butter for brushing
3 tablespoons confectioners' sugar
3 tablespoons grated orange zest
Fresh mint sprigs for garnish

Adapt this recipe to the season by using fresh figs, diced winter pears, or other berries or stone fruit.

Combine the berries, sugar, and liqueur in a bowl; set aside. In a blender, combine the milk, eggs, cornmeal, flour, vanilla, and salt, and blend until smooth. Let the batter rest for 30 minutes. In a 7-inch crepe or omelet pan over medium-high heat, melt ¼ teaspoon of the butter and swirl to coat the surface. Pour in ¼ cup (or less) batter all at once; quickly tilt the pan so the batter flows over the entire surface (don't worry if there are a few holes). Cook until the surface starts to dry and the edges brown, about 1 minute. Turn with a spatula and brown the other side. Turn out onto a plate. Repeat to cook the remaining batter, stirring the batter before cooking each crepe and stacking the cooked crepes. Keep the crepes warm in a low oven.

To serve, warm the berries and their liquid in a skillet over low heat. On each crepe, spread 1 teaspoon apricot jam, then top with 3 to 4 tablespoons berries and 2 tablespoons sour cream and roll. Repeat fill and roll the remaining crepes. Serve 2 crepes on each warm plate. Brush lightly with melted butter and dust with confectioners' sugar. Sprinkle with orange zest and garnish with mint sprig.

MAKES 16 CREPES; SERVES 8

:: *Orange Cake* ::

6 egg yolks
1¾ cups sugar
Pinch of salt
3 tablespoons cold water
1 cup sifted cake flour
1 teaspoon baking powder
1 teaspoon vanilla extract
4 egg whites

ORANGE SYRUP
Grated zest of 2 oranges
¾ cup orange juice
¾ cup sugar
2 egg whites

Whipped cream flavored with sugar
   and vanilla extract to taste

A wonderful, light cake that should be baked one day before serving.

Preheat the oven to 325°F. Butter two 9-inch round cake pans.

   In a large bowl, beat the egg yolks, 1 cup of the sugar, and the salt together. Beat in the cold water, flour, baking powder, and vanilla. In a large bowl, beat the egg whites until stiff, glossy peaks form. Fold the beaten whites into the egg yolk mixture until well blended. Pour into the prepared pans and bake for 35 minutes, or until a cake tester inserted in the center comes out clean.

To make the syrup: In a small bowl, mix the orange zest, juice, and sugar together. In a large bowl, beat the egg whites until soft peaks form. Blend into the orange mixture. Pour over the warm cake and let stand overnight. To serve, frost with the flavored whipped cream.

MAKES ONE 9-INCH 2-LAYER CAKE

:: *Cara's Chocolate Cake* ::

2 cups unbleached all-purpose flour
1 teaspoon baking soda
Pinch of salt
1¾ cups strong coffee
¼ cup bourbon
5 ounces unsweetened chocolate, chopped
1 cup (2 sticks) butter
2 cups sugar
2 eggs, lightly beaten
1 teaspoon vanilla extract

This cake is fairly dense and very chocolaty. It needs no icing, but whipped cream or ice cream is a wonderful addition.

Preheat the oven to 275°F. Grease a 9-inch tube or Bundt pan and dust the inside with unsweetened cocoa powder. Sift the flour, baking soda, and salt together. Set aside. Combine the coffee and bourbon in a double boiler over boiling water. Heat for 5 minutes. Add the chocolate and butter. Stir until melted and smooth. Remove from heat and stir in the sugar. Let cool for 3 minutes.

Transfer to a large mixing bowl. Add the flour mixture, ½ cup at a time, beating until smooth after each addition. (Beat carefully. The batter is thin and tends to splatter.) Beat 1 more minute. Add the eggs and vanilla and mix in thoroughly. Pour into the prepared pan and bake at 275°F for 1 hour and 35 minutes, or until cake pulls away from sides of pan.

SERVES 12

Masami Teraoka, *31 Flavors Invading Japan (Today's Special)*, 1977

:: *Mrs. Rathbone's Chocolate Angel Strata Pie* ::

MERINGUE

2 egg whites

½ teaspoon distilled white vinegar

¼ teaspoon salt

¼ teaspoon ground cinnamon

½ cup sugar

One 9-inch baked pie shell, cooled

CHOCOLATE FILLING

2 egg yolks, lightly beaten

¼ cup water

6 ounces semisweet chocolate, melted

WHIPPED CREAM FILLING

¼ cup sugar

¼ teaspoon ground cinnamon

1 cup heavy cream

This extremely tasty, light dessert takes a bit of time, but is well worth it. It makes a delightful finish to a celebratory meal.

Preheat the oven to 325°F.

To make the meringue: In a large bowl, beat the egg whites, vinegar, salt, and cinnamon together until soft peaks form. Gradually beat in the sugar until stiff, glossy peaks form. Spread on the bottom and up the sides of the pie shell. Bake for 15 to 18 minutes, or until light brown. Let cool.

To make the chocolate filling: Mix the egg yolks and water together. Add to the melted chocolate. Spread 3 tablespoons of the chocolate mixture over the cooled meringue. Cover and refrigerate the remaining mixture.

To make the whipped cream filling: In a deep bowl, beat the sugar, cinnamon, and cream together until stiff peaks form. Spread half of this mixture over the chocolate filling in the pie shell. Add the chilled chocolate mixture to the remaining whipped cream filling. Mix until well blended and spread on top of the pie. Refrigerate for 4 hours.

MAKES ONE 9-INCH PIE

:: *Holiday Cranberry Cake* ::

½ cup (1 stick) plus 1 tablespoon butter
   at room temperature

1 cup sugar

1 egg

¼ teaspoon almond extract

1 cup raisins, soaked in water to plump,
   and drained

2 cups unbleached all-purpose flour

½ teaspoon baking soda

1¼ teaspoons baking powder

1 teaspoon ground cinnamon

¼ teaspoon ground cloves

¼ teaspoon ground allspice

½ teaspoon salt

2 cups (16 ounces) whole-berry
   cranberry sauce

Confectioners' sugar for dusting

The recipe for this festive cake originated in New Hampshire. Serve it alongside the pumpkin pie at Thanksgiving dinner. It's also good glazed with an icing of confectioners' sugar and lemon juice.

Preheat the oven to 350°F. Grease a 9- or 10-inch round springform pan.

In a large bowl, cream the butter and sugar together until fluffy. Beat the egg with the almond extract. Add to creamed mixture and beat again. Add the raisins and mix. Combine the flour, baking soda, baking powder, spices, and salt in a bowl and stir with a fork. Pour into a flour sifter and sift into the creamed mixture. Stir to blend well. Add the cranberry sauce and mix.

Bake in the prepared pan for 1 hour, or until cake tester inserted in the center comes out clean. Let cool slightly and carefully remove the sides and bottom section.

Dust with confectioners' sugar.

MAKES ONE 9- OR 10-INCH CAKE

:: *Cranberry Surprise Pie* ::

2 cups fresh or frozen cranberries
½ cup (2 ounces) chopped pecans
   (do not substitute another nut)
1½ cups sugar
2 eggs
1 cup sifted all-purpose flour
Pinch of salt
¾ cup butter, melted
Vanilla ice cream for serving

Preheat the oven to 325°F. Generously oil a 9-inch pie plate.

In a medium bowl, combine the cranberries, pecans, and ½ cup of the sugar. Pour into the prepared pie plate. In a medium bowl, beat the eggs until thick and pale. Gradually beat in the sugar. Beat in the flour, salt, and butter. Pour over the cranberry mixture.

Bake for 50 minutes, or until golden brown. Cut around the rim before serving. Serve at room temperature, with ice cream.

MAKES ONE 9-INCH PIE; SERVES 6 TO 8

:: *Bavarian Pear Torte* ::

½ cup (1 stick) butter at room
   temperature
⅓ cup plus ¼ cup sugar
¼ teaspoon vanilla extract
¾ cup all-purpose flour
⅔ cup chopped walnuts
8 ounces cream cheese at room
   temperature
1 egg
½ teaspoon vanilla extract
3 ripe pears, peeled, cored, and cut
   into ½-inch-thick slices
1 teaspoon ground cinnamon

This favorite recipe is easy to make and can be done two days ahead of time.

Preheat the oven to 450°F. In a large bowl, cream the butter, ⅓ cup sugar, and vanilla together until light and fluffy. Gradually add the flour and beat until well mixed. Stir in the walnuts. With lightly floured hands, press into a 10-inch springform pan.

In a small bowl, beat the cream cheese with the remaining ¼ cup sugar. Beat in the egg and vanilla and pour into the pan. Place the pears on the cream cheese mixture in a circular design and sprinkle with the cinnamon.

Bake for 10 minutes, then reduce the oven temperature to 400°F and bake for 25 minutes or until lightly browned. Let cool for 10 minutes. Remove the pan sides and let cool completely.

MAKES ONE 10-INCH TORTE

James Peale, *Still Life with Fruit*, ca. 1821

:: *Sweet Potato Pie* ::

PIE CRUST

2 cups self-rising flour

⅔ cup shortening

6 tablespoons cold water

FILLING

2 medium to large sweet potatoes or
yams with pink skin and light orange
flesh, not yellow, peeled and chopped
(4 to 5 cups)

½ cup (1 stick) butter

1 to 1⅓ cups sugar

2 teaspoons ground nutmeg

¾ cup evaporated milk or half-and-half

3 to 4 eggs

A dash of your favorite extract (lemon,
rum, coconut, orange, or vanilla)

To make the pastry: Place the flour in a medium bowl. Using a pastry cutter or 2 knives, cut the shortening into the flour until it resembles coarse meal. Mix in cold water, 1 tablespoon at a time, just until dough holds together. Shape the dough into a ball and flatten into a disk. Wrap in plastic and refrigerate for 30 minutes to 1 hour. Roll out the dough on a lightly floured surface. Transfer to a 9-inch pie plate. Trim and crimp the edges. Set aside.

To make the filling: Cook the yams in salted boiling water for about 30 minutes, or until tender. Drain and put in a bowl. Add the butter, sugar, nutmeg, evaporated milk or half-and-half, eggs, and flavoring and beat until well blended and smooth.

Preheat the oven to 375°F. Pour the filling into the pie crust and bake for 40 to 50 minutes or until a knife inserted in the center comes out clean.

MAKES ONE 9-INCH PIE

*Gelede Helmet Mask Face Topped with
Two Figures Carrying Bread,* Yoruba,
Nigeria, 20th century

:: *Baklava* ::

3⅔ cups (11 ounces) walnuts
¾ cup sugar
2 teaspoons ground cinnamon
1 teaspoon ground allspice
1½ cups (3 sticks) unsalted butter, melted
1 pound frozen phyllo dough, thawed
Whole cloves

HONEY SYRUP
⅔ cup sugar
⅔ cup water
1 cup honey
1¼ teaspoons vanilla extract

This recipe was inspired by a trip to Greece. The baklava is much in demand as a holiday treat.

Preheat the oven to 300°F. Using a large knife or a small hand-cranked nut chopper, chop the walnuts to a medium-fine dice. In a medium bowl, mix the nuts, sugar, cinnamon, and allspice.

Brush the bottom of a 9 × 13-inch baking pan with melted butter. (Keep the butter warm in a double boiler over hot water.) Using 1 phyllo sheet at a time, and keeping the remaining phyllo covered with a damp cloth, cut the phyllo to make 1 layer in the bottom of the pan. Brush with melted butter. Repeat to make 6 layers. Cover with a thin layer of the walnut mixture. Cover with one layer of pastry, brush with butter, and sprinkle with the nut mixture. Continue to alternate 1 pastry sheet brushed with butter, and 1 layer of walnut mixture until you have just enough pastry sheets left to make 6 buttered layers, as at the beginning. Layer and butter the dough.

With a sharp knife dipped in the hot butter, cut the baklava into strips 1½ inches wide, and cut these strips diagonally to form small diamond-shaped pieces. Stick a clove into the center of each piece. Pour the remaining butter into the knife slits between the strips. Bake for about 1 hour, or until lightly browned.

After the baklava has baked for about 40 minutes, start making the syrup: In a heavy, medium saucepan, cook the sugar and water over low heat until syrupy, about 10 minutes. Add the honey and vanilla and cook for 5 minutes. Slowly pour enough boiling hot syrup to cover the surface of the baklava. Increase the oven temperature to 400°F and return to the oven for a few minutes longer or until the syrup has penetrated and the top is golden brown. Remove and pour as much of the remaining syrup over the top as it will absorb. Let stand for about 45 minutes, or until still slightly warm, and remove in large sections to a clean pan to finish cooling completely, about 2 more hours.

Note: Measure the 1 cup of honey in an oiled 2-cup measure

MAKES 48 PIECES

:: *Kourabides (Greek Butter Cookies)* ::

2 cups (4 sticks) unsalted butter at
    room temperature
¾ cup confectioners' sugar, sifted,
    plus ¼ cup more for coating
1 teaspoon vanilla extract
2 tablespoons brandy or Cognac
2 egg yolks
5 cups unbleached all-purpose flour
½ cup ground walnuts or almonds
    (optional)

This is an old family recipe.

Preheat the oven to 300°F. Lightly grease baking sheets or line them with parchment paper.

In a large bowl, beat the butter until it is fluffy and pale in color. Add the ¾ cup sugar, the vanilla, and brandy or Cognac and beat well. Add the yolks, mixing in well. Gradually stir in the flour and then the nuts, if using. Shape by teaspoonfuls into ovals about ⅜-inch thick, place on the prepared pans, and form into crescents. The cookies can be placed fairly close together as they don't spread very much. Bake until very lightly colored, about 45 minutes.

Meanwhile, sift confectioners' sugar onto a sheet of waxed paper. When the cookies are done, transfer them, while still hot, onto the sugar and dust the tops heavily. Let cool on wire racks.

MAKES 4 DOZEN COOKIES

:: *Cheesecake* ::

8 ounces cream cheese at room
   temperature
12 ounces cottage cheese
6 large eggs, separated
1 cup sugar
2 cups (16 ounces) sour cream
1 tablespoon vanilla extract
Pinch of salt
3 heaping tablespoons cornstarch

You can cut the calories considerably in this airy, custardy cake by substituting low-fat (but not nonfat) versions of the dairy ingredients.

Preheat the oven to 425°F. Wrap the bottom of a 10-inch round springform pan with heavy-duty aluminum foil to ensure a tight fit when the side section is attached.

In a large bowl, beat the cream cheese and cottage cheese together until thoroughly mixed. Beat in the egg yolks one at a time. Beat in the sugar, and then the sour cream, vanilla, and salt. In a small bowl, mix the cornstarch with enough of the batter to make a smooth paste. Add the cornstarch mixture to the batter and beat until smooth. In a large bowl, beat the egg whites until stiff, glossy peaks form. Mix one-fourth of the egg whites into the batter to lighten it, then gently fold in the rest.

Pour the batter into the prepared pan. Place the pan in a baking pan and pour hot water into the baking pan to halfway up the sides of the springform pan. Bake for 5 minutes. Reduce heat to 275°F and bake for about 70 minutes, or until cheesecake is nearly set; the center will still jiggle slightly when the pan is shaken. Run a knife around the edge of the cake and return the pan to the turned-off oven. Leave the door completely open and let the cake cool for 1 hour. Cover and refrigerate for at least 4 hours or preferably for 1 day before serving.

SERVES 10 TO 12

Steuben Toasting Goblet with Air-Twist Stem, New York, 1961

:: *Molasses Cookies* ::

¾ cup (1½ sticks) butter or margarine
1 cup granulated sugar
¼ cup dark molasses
1 egg
2 cups unbleached all-purpose flour
2 teaspoons baking soda
½ teaspoon ground cloves
½ teaspoon ground ginger
1 teaspoon ground cinnamon
½ teaspoon salt
Sifted confectioners' sugar for coating

Preheat the oven to 375°F. Grease baking sheets or line them with parchment paper.

In a large saucepan, melt the butter over low heat. Let cool. Add the sugar, molasses, and egg to the butter. Beat well. In a medium bowl, mix the flour, baking soda, spices, and salt together. Stir into the molasses mixture and mix well.

Cover and refrigerate for at least 2 hours or overnight. Form the chilled dough into 1-inch balls and roll in confectioners' sugar. Place on the prepared pans and bake for 8 to 10 minutes. Let cool on pan for 1 minute, then transfer to a wire rack to cool.

MAKES ABOUT 3 DOZEN COOKIES

:: *Gingersnaps* ::

¾ cup shortening
1 cup brown sugar
1 egg
¼ cup molasses
2 cups all-purpose flour
2 teaspoons baking soda
¼ teaspoon salt
1 teaspoon ground ginger
1 teaspoon ground cloves
1 teaspoon ground cinnamon
½ cup chopped candied (crystallized) ginger
raw sugar for coating

Martin Guillaume Biennais, *Hot Water Urn*, 1809–19

With a few changes, molasses cookies become gingersnaps.

Preheat the oven to 350°F. Grease baking sheets or line them with parchment paper.

In a large bowl, beat the shortening and the 1 cup sugar together. Add the egg and beat until light and fluffy, then add the molasses. In a medium bowl, stir the flour, baking soda, salt, ginger, cloves, and cinnamon together; add to the first mixture, beating until smooth and blended. Add the crystallized ginger and mix thoroughly. Using your hands, roll the dough into 1-inch balls, then roll each ball in raw sugar to coat evenly. Place about 2 inches apart on prepared pans and bake for 10 to 12 minutes, or until set and lightly browned.

MAKES ABOUT 40 COOKIES

:: *Aunt Martha's Peppermint Squares* ::

CAKE

1 cup milk

2 ounces unsweetened chocolate, chopped

1 tablespoon butter or shortening

1 cup sugar

⅓ teaspoon salt

1½ cups sifted unbleached all-purpose flour

1 teaspoon baking soda

3 tablespoons boiling water

1 teaspoon vanilla extract

FROSTING

4 cups (1 pound) confectioners' sugar

6 tablespoons butter

½ teaspoon salt

2 teaspoons peppermint extract

4 to 5 tablespoons milk (to spreading consistency)

Green food coloring

TOPPING

3 ounces unsweetened chocolate, chopped

1 tablespoon butter

This delicious cookie was a childhood favorite. Great with cool milk on a hot day.

To make the cake: Preheat the oven to 350°F. Butter a 10 × 15-inch jellyroll pan.

In a large saucepan, heat ½ cup of the milk with the chocolate until the chocolate melts; beat until smooth and thick. Add the butter, sugar, salt, and flour. Dissolve the baking soda in the water and add to the mixture. Stir in the remaining ½ cup milk and the vanilla. Pour into the prepared pan and bake for 10 minutes, or until a toothpick inserted in the center comes out clean. Let cool.

To make the frosting: Mix all the frosting ingredients together and spread over the cake. Let the frosting set.

To make the topping: In a double boiler over barely simmering water, melt the chocolate and butter together. Spread evenly over the top of the frosted cake. Cut into squares.

MAKES 30 SQUARES

Brocade Pomegranate (detail), Italy, ca. 1739

:: *Almond Ginger Cookies* ::

½ cup blanched almonds

¼ cup candied (crystallized) ginger

½ cup (1 stick) unsalted butter at
　room temperature

1 cup sugar

1 egg

½ teaspoon almond extract

½ teaspoon salt

1 teaspoon baking powder

1 cup all-purpose flour

These are good served with fresh berries or fruit salad. Even people who virtuously watch their calorie and cholesterol intake will love these cookies.

Preheat the oven to 375°F. In a food processor, separately chop the almonds and ginger and set aside. Cream the butter and sugar together in the food processor. Add in the egg and process. Return the nuts and ginger to the processor, add the remaining ingredients, and process until well mixed. The batter will be a bit lumpy. Drop teaspoonfuls 2 inches apart on ungreased baking sheets. Flatten slightly with the bottom of a cup or glass that has been dipped in sugar.

　Bake until the edges of the cookies are brown, 8 to 10 minutes. Let cool for about 3 minutes, then transfer to wire racks using a wide spatula.

MAKES ABOUT 3 DOZEN COOKIES

Wayne Thiebaud, *Candy Apples*, 1987

:: *Ginger Shortbread Cookies* ::

2 cups unbleached all-purpose flour

½ cup cornstarch

½ cup plus 2 tablespoons superfine sugar

½ teaspoon ground ginger

1 cup (2 sticks) unsalted butter at room temperature

4 ounces candied (crystallized) ginger, chopped

Preheat the oven to 250°F. Line a baking sheet with parchment paper or use a double-bottomed baking sheet.

Sift the flour, cornstarch, sugar, and ground ginger together into a medium bowl. Place the butter in a large bowl and gradually stir in the flour mixture until it is too stiff to stir, then work it in with your hands. Add the candied ginger and work it in. Turn the dough out onto a floured board and knead until the mixture cracks, adding more flour 1 tablespoon at a time, if necessary, to prevent sticking. Divide the dough in half. Roll out one half into a rectangle about ⅜-inch thick and cut into 24 squares. Place 1 inch apart on a prepared pan. Repeat with the second piece of dough. (The dough can also be rolled into 2 rounds and left uncut. Crimp the edges, score for cutting later, and prick the centers. Cut into wedges while still warm.)

Bake for 30 to 45 minutes, or until delicately colored. Let cool on the pan. They will become crisper as they cool.

:: *Hazelnut Shortbread*

Substitute ¼ cup packed brown sugar for ¼ cup of the superfine sugar. Omit the ground ginger. Substitute 1 cup chopped peeled hazelnuts for the candied ginger. 1 teaspoon Frangelico liqueur may be added, if you like.

MAKES 4 DOZEN COOKIES

:: *Lemon Squares* ::

BASE

2 cups unsifted flour

½ cup sifted confectioners' sugar

1 cup (2 sticks) cold butter, cut into
small pieces

TOPPING

4 eggs

2 cups sugar

¼ cup flour

1 teaspoon grated lemon zest

¼ cup fresh lemon juice

Confectioners' sugar for dusting

These cookies always elicit recipe requests from people. They look like a fancy dessert, but are easy to make.

Preheat the oven to 350°F. In a medium bowl, combine the flour and sugar. With a pastry blender or 2 knives, cut the butter into the flour mixture until it resembles coarse meal. Press the mixture into a 9 × 13-inch metal baking pan. (Don't use dark metal.) Bake on the center rack of the oven for 20 minutes, or until golden, but not brown.

To make the topping: In a medium bowl, beat the eggs and stir in the sugar and flour just until mixed. Add the zest and juice. When the base is done, immediately pour the topping over the hot base, return to the oven, and bake for 20 to 25 minutes, or until the center of the topping is set but yields slightly to the touch. Sift confectioners' sugar over the hot cookies. Let cool in the pan on a rack. Cut into 2-inch squares.

MAKES THIRTY-TWO 2-INCH-SQUARE COOKIES

Works of Art Illustrated

All works illustrated are a part of the collections or on long-term loan to the Fine Arts Museums of San Francisco.

Cover
William J. McCloskey
American, 1859–1941
Oranges in Tissue Paper (detail), ca. 1890
Oil on canvas, 10 × 17 in.
Gift of Mr. and Mrs. John D. Rockefeller 3rd, 1993.35.21

Title page
John Singer Sargent
American, b. Italy, 1856–1925
A Dinner Table at Night (The Glass of Claret) (detail), 1884
Oil on canvas, 20¼ × 26¼ in.
Gift of the Atholl McBean Foundation, 73.12

p. 6
Charles Sheeler
American, 1883–1965
Kitchen, Williamsburg, 1937
Oil on hardboard, 10 × 14 in.
Gift of Mr. and Mrs. John D. Rockefeller 3rd, 1993.35.24

Effigy Beaker, North Coast Peru,
A.D. 1200

p. 8
Albrecht Dürer
German, 1471–1528
Adam and Eve, 1504
Engraving, 10 × 7 ¾ in.
Achenbach Foundation for Graphic Arts, gift of Thomas Carr Howe, Jr., 1953.42

p. 13
Anonymous, Japanese
Radishes and Summer Herbs, ca. 1820–35
Color woodcut surimono, 8¹/₁₆ × 7⅛ in.
Achenbach Foundation for Graphic Arts purchase, 1982.1.106

p. 15
Wallpaper (detail)
From *The Voyages of Captain Cook*
French, Mâcon, 1804–6
Designed by Jean Gabriel Charvet, 1750–1829
Printed by Joseph Dufour, 1752–1827
Block print on paper
Gift of Georgia M. Worthington and The Fine Arts Museums Trustees Fund, 77.6.1–20

p. 21
Ronald Searle
English, b. 1920
Right!, drawing for page 25 of the booklet
How to Open a Bottle of Wine (Clos du Val and Taltarni: 1983), 1982
Pen and black ink, colored pencils, and watercolor on wove paper mounted to heavier sheet, 11³/₁₆ × 8⁵/₁₆ in.
Achenbach Foundation for Graphic Arts, gift of John Goelet, 1987.2.66

p. 49
Charles Jones
English, 1868–1959
Runner Beans, ca. 1900
Gelatin silver print, 8¼ × 5⁵⁄₁₆ in.
Achenbach Foundation for Graphic Arts
purchase, 1996.105

p. 52
Roy Lichtenstein
American, 1923–1997
Sandwich and Soda, from the portfolio *Ten
Works/Ten Painters*
Published by the Wadsworth Atheneum, 1964
Color screenprint on clear plastic film, 19 × 23 in.
Achenbach Foundation for Graphic Arts
purchase, 1976.1.431.7

pp. 54–55
Virgil Solis
German, 1514–1562
Hares Roasting a Hunter, 16th century
Engraving, 1½ × 8 in.
Achenbach Foundation for Graphic Arts
purchase, 1969.32.8

p. 56
Storage Basket
Yokuts, Tulare County, California, early
20th century
Muhlenbergia grass, sedge, bracken fern, and
redbud, H. 11 in., DIAM: 22 in.
Gift of Mr. H. H. Welsh, 51961.8

p. 58
Thomas Waterman Wood
American, 1823–1903
Market Woman, 1858
Oil on canvas, 23⅜ × 14½ in.
Mildred Anna Williams Collection, 1944.8

p. 62
Mark Adams
American, b. 1925
Eggplant, 1978
Watercolor, 23 × 17 in.
Achenbach Foundation for Graphic Arts,
Hamilton-Wells Fund, 1978.2.29

p. 65
Lion-Shaped Rhyton (Libation Vessel)
Anatolian, Kanish (Kültepe), *karum* period,
ca. 1860–1780 B.C.
Terracotta, H. 7⅝ in.
Gift of the Queen of Greece through Alma
de Bretteville Spreckels, 1924.15

p. 68
Jerome Thompson
American, 1814–1886
Recreation (detail), 1857
Oil on canvas, 40½ × 56 in.
Museum purchase, 47.13

p. 71
Bowls (Umeke)
Hawaiian Islands, 18th–19th century
Koa wood, H. 8½ in., DIAM: 10¾ in.; H. 7 in.,
DIAM: 5¾ in.
Gift of Mary Taylor Beardsley, 47.23.1 and 5

p. 72
*Bowl in the Form of a Squash Supported by
Standing Men*
Colima, Mexico, 200 B.C.–A.D. 300
Ceramic, 10 × 14 in.
Lent by the Land Collection, L1994.3.9

p. 75
Glen Baxter
British, b. 1944
The Fourth Time, 1984
Color lithograph, 17¾ × 19¾ in.
Achenbach Foundation for Graphic Arts
purchase, 1986.1.8

Works of Art Illustrated

p. 76
Wesley Chamberlin
American, 1932–1990
Seagram's, 1974
Color linocut, 16½ × 22⅝ in.
Achenbach Foundation for Graphic Arts,
Hamilton-Wells Fund, 1981.1.14

p. 78
The Last Supper (detail), from *Scenes from the
Life of Christ*
Flemish (Brussels) tapestry, ca. 1510
Warp: undyed wool, 6 per cm; weft: dyed wool
and silk, 5 ft. 10 in. × 20 ft.
Roscoe and Margaret Oakes Collection,
museum purchase by exchange, gift of various
donors, 1976.3

p. 81
Arnold Genthe
American, 1869–1942
The Vegetable Peddler from *The Chinatown Series*,
ca. 1896
Gelatin silver print, 8¹⁵⁄₁₆ × 11⅞ in.
Achenbach Foundation for Graphic Arts,
A045830

pp. 82–83
Grant Wood
American, 1891–1942
Dinner for Threshers, 1934
Oil on hardboard, 20 × 80 in.
Gift of Mr. and Mrs. John D. Rockefeller 3rd,
1979.7.105

p. 85
Eugène Feuillatre
French, 1870–1916
Vase with Base in the Form of an Artichoke,
ca. 1900
Enamel on silver, 5½ × 3 in.
Gift of Golden Gate Collectors, 1991.11

p. 86
Rabbit-Hunting with Ferrets (detail)
Franco-Flemish (probably Tournai) tapestry,
1460–70
Warp: undyed wool, 6 per cm; weft: dyed wool
and silk, 10 ft. × 11 ft. 11 in.
Gift of M. H. de Young Endowment Fund,
39.4.1

p. 90
Porringer and Stand
English, London, 1662
Made by R. F.
Silver, H. of porringer 8 in., DIAM. of stand
16½ in.
Roscoe and Margaret Oakes Collection, 76.4a–c

p. 95
Jean-Baptiste Oudry
French, 1686–1755
The Pâté, 1743
Oil on canvas, 69¾ × 49 in.
Mildred Anna Williams Collection, 1956.91

p. 98
Aquamanile (Ewer)
German, Hildesheim, ca. 1400
Bronze, H. 9⅝ in.
Purchased with funds from various donors, 54.22

p. 101
Relief from the Tomb of Mentuemhet
Egyptian, Thebes, 25th–26th Dynasties,
ca. 660 B.C.
Limestone with polychrome, H. 14 in.
Museum purchase, M. H. de Young Memorial
Museum, 51.4.2

p. 102
Edwin Deakin
American, b. England, 1838–1923
Flame Tokay Grapes, 1884
Oil on canvas, 30 × 20 in.
Gift of Charles Hirsch, 42084

p. 105
David Gilhooly
American, b. 1943
My Daily Bread, 1983
Color monoprint, 24 × 42¾ in.
Anderson Graphic Arts Collection, gift of
the Harry W. and Mary Margaret Anderson
Charitable Foundation, 1996.74.146

p. 106
David Lance Goines
American, b. 1945
EAT, 1980
Color offset lithograph poster, 22 × 14⅞ in.
Achenbach Foundation for Graphic Arts,
Frank M. Carlson Memorial Collection, gift of
the artist and Thackrey and Robertson, 1981.1.45

p. 109
Arnold Genthe
American, 1869–1942
A Sidewalk Kitchen, 1906
Gelatin silver print, 10⁷⁄₁₆ × 13¼ in.
Achenbach Foundation for Graphic Arts,
A046260

p. 110
Red-Figure Hydria (Water Jar)
Greek, Athens, ca. 480–450 B.C.
Attributed to the Pan Painter
Terracotta, H. 10¾ in.
California Midwinter International Exposition
through M. H. de Young, 707

p. 112
Gunter Grass
German, b. 1927
Man in Flounder (Mann im Butt), 1978
Etching, 15½ × 20⅛ in.
Achenbach Foundation for Graphic Arts
purchase, 1981.1.5

p. 114
Jasper Johns
American, b. 1930
Bread, 1969
Sheet lead relief, embossed rag paper, hand-
painted by the artist, 23 × 17 in.
Anderson Graphic Arts Collection, gift of
the Harry W. and Mary Margaret Anderson
Charitable Foundation, 1996.74.215

p. 120
Pair of Plates
English, Worcester, 1780–85
Soft-paste porcelain, DIAM: 8½ in.
Gift of Constance Crowley Bowles,
1991.40.13.1–2

p. 123
Nicolas Lancret
French, 1690–1743
Breakfast before the Hunt, ca. 1740
Oil on canvas (lunette), 24 × 52½ in.
Gift of Mrs. William Hayward, 53.2.2

p. 125
Goblet
English, London, 1590
Workshop of Giacomo Verzelini (1522–1606)
Glass, H: 7¼ in.
The Franz W. Sichel Foundation, 1988.15.58

p. 126
Fichu (detail)
French, 1700–20
Point de France lace, linen, 12¼ × 65 in.
Gift of Mrs. D. L. Wemple, 77.24.13

p. 129
Wayne Thiebaud
American, b. 1920
Lunch, 1967
Etching with watercolor additions by the artist,
5 × 6¹³⁄₁₆ in.
Achenbach Foundation for Graphic Arts,
Hamilton-Wells Fund, 1978.1.34

p. 130
Peter Carl Fabergé
Russian, 1846–1920
Tea Service and Table
Russian, St. Petersburg, 1896–1908
Workmaster: Julius Rappaport (1864–1918)
Silver; table veneered in karelian birch, L. 30 in.
Gift of Victoria Melita, Grand Duchess Kiril,
through Alma de Bretteville Spreckels,
1945.355–366

p. 133
Paul Storr
English, 1771–1844
One of a Pair of Sauceboats, 1819
Silver, 6½ × 4½ × 10 in.
Roscoe and Margaret Oakes Collection, 70.22.2

p. 134
J. Paul Verrees
American, active 20th century
The Kaiser Is Canned—Can Food, 1918
Color lithograph poster, 33 × 22¼ in.
Museum purchase, Achenbach Foundation for
Graphic Arts purchase, 1997.116

p. 138
Raphaelle Peale
American, 1774–1825
Blackberries (detail), ca. 1813
Oil on wood panel, 7¼ × 10¼ in.
Gift of Mr. and Mrs. John D. Rockefeller 3rd,
1993.35.23

p. 143
Anne Vallayer-Coster
French, 1744–1818
Still Life with Plums and a Lemon, 1778
Oil on canvas, 16⅜ × 18⅝ in.
Gift of Mr. and Mrs. Louis A. Benoist, 1960.30

p. 144
Bertha Lum
American, 1879–1954
Green Dragon Cocktail, 1937
Color woodcut, 12¹⁵⁄₁₆ × 9⅛ in.
Achenbach Foundation for Graphic Arts, gift
of Mr. and Mrs. Edouard J. Bourbousson,
1962.77.68

p. 146
Vessel for Drinking Chocolate
Maya, Petén, Guatemala, A.D. 600
Polychrome ceramic, 7 × 5 in.
Museum purchase, Salinger Fund, 78.41

p. 150
Masami Teraoka
American, b. Japan, 1936
31 Flavors Invading Japan (Today's Special), 1977
Color woodcut, 10⅜ × 15¾ in.
Achenbach Foundation for Graphic Arts, gift of
Edward Den Lau, 1996.92.3

p. 154
James Peale
American, 1749–1831
Still Life with Fruit, ca. 1821
Oil on panel, 18¼ × 25¼ in.
Museum purchase, 46.11

p. 157
*Gelede Helmet Mask Face Topped with Two
Figures Carrying Bread*
Yoruba, Nigeria, Africa, 20th century
Wood and cord, H. 19½ in., DIAM: 10 in.
Museum purchase, 71.20

p. 161
Toasting Goblet with Air-Twist Stem
American, 1961
Manufacturer: Steuben Glass Works, Corning, New York
Lead glass, h. 18 in.
Gift of Judith and Robert Shaw, 1991.5.1

p. 162
Martin Guillaume Biennais
French, 1764–1843
Hot Water Urn, 1809–19
Silver gilt, 17½ × 8½ × 12¼ in.
Gift of Alma de Bretteville Spreckels, 1944.11

p. 165
Brocade (detail)
Italy, ca. 1739
Polychrome silk and silver, 20½ × 93 in.
Museum purchase, Art Trust Fund, 1995.19.2

p. 167
Wayne Thiebaud
American, b. 1920
Candy Apples, 1987
Color woodcut, 15¼ × 16½ in.
Achenbach Foundation for Graphic Arts, Crown Point Press Archive, gift of Crown Point Press, 1992.167.270

p. 170
Effigy Beaker
Lambayeque Valley region, North Coast Peru, A.D. 1200
Gold, 5¾ × 4½ in.
Gift of Mrs. John Wise in memory of Eleanor de Guigne, 1983.25

Back cover flap
Ken Price
American, b. 1935
Untitled, second plate from the portfolio *Heat Wave,* 1995
Screenprint, 10 × 7½ in.
Achenbach Foundation for Graphic Arts, gift of Thomas Lundstrom through the Artist Book Council, 1996.95.2

Acknowledgments

The Art Lover's Cookbook: A Feast for the Eye grew from the generosity of the many people whose names are listed here. Without them there would be no book at all, and with their contributions we have recipes and ideas for cookbooks to come. A committee put this enterprise in motion, but the unflagging attention of Kay Millar and Martha Steen kept it alive. They devoted great time and energy to working with the much-appreciated food consultants Shirley Sarvis and Birgit Skoldberg and those who tested recipes, bringing shape to this first such publication for the Museums. The painstaking work of Cheryl Jeung and Josephine Palmer, and later Eileen Petersen, prepared the manuscript.

The members of the Cookbook Committee, who initiated the project, are indicated in this list, as are the curators who took the time to help with illustrations. On the copyright page the production notes tell you who brought the cookbook to its handsome completion. Finally, Melissa Leventon deserves special mention for more than her hours of help with the book. Her imaginative curatorship of the exhibition *A Feast for the Eye: Food in Art* provided the perfect moment to introduce *The Art Lover's Cookbook* to its waiting public.

H.S.P. III

COOKBOOK COMMITTEE†
CURATORS*

Donna Adams	June Baggiani
Ann Anderson	Rita M. Baldelli
Virginia K. Anderson	Alice Baldocchi
Jerianne Asedo	Norma Baldocchi
Mary Assily	Linda Barry
Doris Austin	Linda Bayford

Jeanne C. Bean

Consuelo Benney

Kathy Berrin*

Lorraine Banas Berry

Ruth Berson

Mary Anne Bewsher

Elizabeth Blake

Chotsie Blank

Peggy Blatchford

Rhea Bogdanoff

Lesley Bone

Dori Bonn

Robert E. Bouchard

Maureen Bourbin

Betty Branstad

Mary Jo Brazil

Karin Breuer*

Sandra Brickman

Inez Brock

Maggie Brosnan

Judy Brush

Sally Bush

Marijke Bych-Hoenselaars

Alyce C. Caley

Jean Chaitin

Therese Chen

Gladys Cherry

Keller Cherry

Louise Chu

Linda Cimmet

Diane Ciucci

Peggy Clemens

Eleanor Cohen

Catherine Ann Colby

Maude Crawford

Robin Crew

Dorothy Cronan

Dorothy Cunningham

Beatrice D'Acosta

Diana Dalton

Mary L. Daly

Marcia Davey

Polly Day

Beverly Denenberg

Jean Dew

J. Diblin

David W. Dippel

Mrs. Frank Draeger

Renée Dreyfus*

Trudy Duncan

Gloria Edson

Judy Edwards

Bobbe Eldridge

Holly Erickson

Connie Ewy

Marya Fan

Marianne Fanelli

Marny Farrell

Louise J. Fellows

Alice Fischer

Jane Flahavan

James Forbes

Pamela Forbes

Cynthia Foster

Eleanore Foster†

Janet Fouts

Franklin A. Franco

Donald Frediani

Dorothy Free

Louise Friedman

Betty Gardner

Sarah Gates†

Julia Geist

Barbara George

Eleanore George

Bernice Giansiracusa

Marcia Goodman

Ted Greenberg

Janet Griggs

Joanne Hackett

Betty Ham

Holly B. Hanson

Judith Harris

Robert Haycock

Mary Helfrich

Beth Hensperger

Jo Q. Hill

Candy Hisert

Kathe Hodgson

Marcia Holm

Annette Holmes

Barbara Holt

Carolyn J. Hughes

Jeanette Huie

Chris Huson

Al Hutson

Carol J. Huvane

Mrs. Tempe Javitz

Anita M. Jepsen

Robert Flynn Johnson*

Patti Junker*

Mary Kane

Ann Heath Karlstrom†

Mary Lou Kemper

Karen Kevorkian†

Joan Kientz

Judy Taylor Kimball

Alice King

Dorothy Kirkonis

Rita Kirkovics

Melissa Klar

Marion S. Knowles

Kazuko Kobara

Susan Koenig

Gary Kong

Paula Kotakis

Barbara A. Kozlowski

Margarita L. Lacey

Ann Lacher

Gennine Lalanne

Maria Lane

Alys Coyle Larson

Guy Le Breton

Janet Lehman

Melissa Leventon*

Frances Lilienthal

Gail Lindlow

Emily Lolley

Jean Otto Loomis

Nancy Luke

Delores Malone

Lin E. Mangiante

Barbara Marks

Jean Clark Marks

Brian Marston

Dana Martin-Newman

Ann Reynolds Mason

Patricia Mattox

Christine McCullough

Joseph McDonald

Leah B. McDonough

Vicki McKale

Mrs. Bruce McKleroy

Gloria Melone

Joan Meltesen

Peter R. Mikklesen

Kay Millar†

Lee Hunt Miller†*

Katie Millhiser

Pauline Mohr

Betty Moran

Anita Motta

Kathy Murphy

Lauren Nakagawa

Carol Nash

Dorothy Ann Nelson

Jane Nelson

Robert Nelson

Wanda Nervi

Vera Nusbaum

Rick O'Connell

Anne O'Donnell

Jean O'Donnell

Marnay O'Neal

Lynn Federle Orr*

Josephine Palmer

Sally Palmer

Ellen Parker

Katherine Parkes

Kay Payne

Stuart Peckham

Eileen Petersen

Suzy Peterson†

Adrienne Pierucci

Tracy Power

Joan Prime

Sonja Pröitz

Pautie Azerbaijani Purnell

Susan Reichert

Tutt Remak

Patricia Reynolds

Sandi Roorda

Toby Rose

Stephanie Ross

Maxine Rosston

Ann Ryan

Elizabeth Ryan
Nan Sabino
Michael Sandgren
Mary Jane Sargent
Dori Sassin
Pat Sax
Renate Hunziker Scapin
Jean Scardina
Agneta Schipper
Kate Schlafly†
Maie Kimball Schlafly
Norma Schlossman
Judy Schneider
Janice Schopfer
Delores Schweizer
Mary Ide Secrest
P. Segal (Roberta Pizzimenti)
Vivien Sherman
Fronia Simpson
Marc Simpson
Marian Schell Skiles
Barbara Smitt
Martha Steen†
Phyllis Stephens
Hazel Stitt

Phil Stockhausen
Juliet Rose Tessicini
Marilyn Thompson
Jane Thurston
Hazel Toepfer
Teddy N. Toklas
Mary Louise Tomblin
Rhoda Tracey
Barbara Traisman†
Margueritte Travaillé
Cara Varnell
Turid Vizcarra
Sylvia Solochek Walters
Lorraine Weaver
Estelle Weintraub
Arthur Welch
Milah Russia Wermer
Ellen C. Hvatum Werner
Milka Wigfield
Cynthia Wolfe
Silvana Wong
Margaret Yung
Peggy Zeigler
Anonymous Contributors

Index

Index

186

Index

Index

Index